T0146786

Grace to Love

A True Story of Faith, Hope and Love

Rhonda Lynn Goff

authorHOUSE®

AuthorHouse™
1663 Liberty Drive
Bloomington, IN 47403
www.authorhouse.com
Phone: 1 (800) 839-8640

Published by AuthorHouse   02/24/2016

ISBN: 978-1-5049-7831-6 (sc)
ISBN: 978-1-5049-7830-9 (hc)
ISBN: 978-1-5049-7818-7 (e)

Library of Congress Control Number: 2016902064

Print information available on the last page.

The dedication place of honor for the writing of this book goes to my heavenly Father, the Almighty God in Heaven and to my Lord and Savior, Jesus Christ. I want to openly and publicly offer my gratitude to the Lord for leading and helping me during the process of writing this book. This true story is only made possible for me to share, because the Lord gave me comfort and strength to reduce my experiences to paper to bring honor, praise and glory to His Great Name. May You, heavenly Father, always be glorified through Your Son, Jesus Christ, and may Your love be reflected through my life, ministry and testimony. You are the One who was, who is and is to come. I love you, Lord.

Contents

Preface

It is my prayerful desire that my true story will help strengthen every person who has ever felt lost, abandoned, broken, bruised, rejected, hopeless or defeated. Maybe you are a Jew or a Gentile, and are wondering if a Messiah or Deliverer will ever show up in your circumstances.

I am here to declare to you that there is a God who loves you, who is trustworthy. A God who can mend even the most broken of hearts. There is a God who can heal past and present pain. A God who wants you to know that His love for you will never end; it knows no boundaries, is immeasurable and will last forever.

It's my deepest prayer that as you read this book, there will be an outpouring of the Holy Spirit into your soul and inner most being to reveal Truth to you. I believe God, the One and only true God, the Maker of the heavens and the earth, to bring you supernatural revelation of His great love for you. May you receive by faith, a supernatural impartation of God's divine love, and His divine deliverance over your life. As my story unfolds, you will begin seeing a tiny glimmer of hope for your own life. You will begin to realize that it's not too late for you. You can have hope. You will receive a brand new level of confidence, and begin taking steps to walk in your new found freedom.

May the God of all hope bring you joy and peace, as you really open your heart to begin trusting and believing in His great love for you (see Romans 15:13).

The Lord God calls the brokenhearted. He is inviting you to enter into His arms, receive His love, and be free from your past guilt, mistakes, reckless decisions and former shame.

For I have (like the Apostle Paul) been crucified with Christ, nevertheless I live. Yet not I, but Christ lives within me. This life that I now live in the flesh, in this world, I truly live by the faith of the Son of God. He loves us, and has given His life for us. I refuse to frustrate God's Grace, for if my righteousness is granted by my keeping of The Law, then Jesus Christ died in vain (see Galatians 2:20-21).

The LORD hath appeared of old unto me saying, "Yea, I have loved thee with an everlasting love: therefore with loving kindness have I drawn thee" (Jeremiah 31:3).

"Call unto Me, and I will answer thee, and show you great and mighty things, which thou knowest not" (Jeremiah 33:3).

"For I know the thoughts I think toward you," saith the Lord, "thoughts of peace and not of evil, to give you an expected end, a hopeful future" (Jeremiah 29:11).

If there is any unbearable pain from your past or in your present circumstances, you qualify for a miracle. I may not know your level of pain, but I do know the One who is the miracle Creator God. He makes all things new; He is my miracle Way Maker.

Rhonda Lynn Goff

Acknowledgments

I would like to thank my father and mother, Mr. and Mrs. Charles Kirkendall, for encouraging me to always pursue my dreams, and telling me repeatedly that I could do anything I set my mind to. Dad, I miss you, and know you are cheering me on in the grandstands of Heaven. I will see you one day, and give you a great big hug! Mom, you are the greatest mother in the world, and I am so glad God gave you to me to love and nurture me. Thank you for always being there for me when I needed you most with your unconditional love.

I also want to extend a very special thanks to my best girlfriend, Lori Staas, who without compromise or wavering has given me hope, encouragement and strength over the years. When all else seemed to be failing in my life, thank you, girlfriend, you were always there for me with words of wisdom and counsel. Thank you for consistently partnering with me through prayer, surrounding me with faith filled words, and demonstrating God's love. You are mighty, bold, courageous, strong and beautiful in the Lord. I see you walking daily in your freedom, bringing glory to God.

My sincere gratitude also goes out to Pastor Billy Burke World Outreach. Pastor Billy, thank you for laying down your life as an offering and sacrifice to fulfill the wonderful call of God upon your life. The Lord's anointing is so evident upon you and your ministry. You have spoken countless prophetic words over me, and have given me hope in some of my darkest hours. Thank you for being such a mighty man of God. Your healing and miracle ministry is authentic, and I personally have seen and experienced miracles first hand operated by the gifts of the Holy Spirit through you. To God be all the glory, and may Jesus be lifted high! I praise the Lord for using you to help point me to Jesus when circumstances have contradicted God's plan for my life.

A great big thank you also goes to Eric Ankner, our very talented wedding photographer, who captured some of the most precious moments for us on our special day. We are most grateful!

Lastly, I want to say thank you to my first and only true love, my last love, Mike Goff. You are the only man in the world who has ever been able to reach me on a deep level of understanding. You know how to touch my heart in special ways that only you can. Thank you for being a strong leader, a generous giver, a Christ follower, and a man after God's own heart. There is no deceit in your heart or in your mouth, and the Lord has validated you as genuine. Thank you for being my very best friend. Thank you for being the man of God that follows after Him in truth, holiness, purity and righteousness. No one could ever have what we have, because no one has ever walked where we've walked. We have paid a very high price to be where we are at, and triumphantly have overcome being tragically separated through the devil's lies. We now have the truth. It's been settled. You were my Babe in 1986, and you still are today. I will always love you, and only you, Babe.

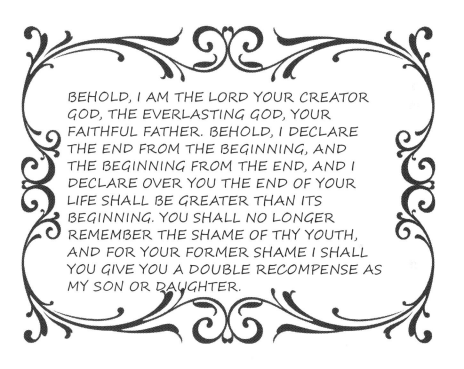

BEHOLD, I AM THE LORD YOUR CREATOR
GOD, THE EVERLASTING GOD, YOUR
FAITHFUL FATHER. BEHOLD, I DECLARE
THE END FROM THE BEGINNING, AND
THE BEGINNING FROM THE END, AND I
DECLARE OVER YOU THE END OF YOUR
LIFE SHALL BE GREATER THAN ITS
BEGINNING. YOU SHALL NO LONGER
REMEMBER THE SHAME OF THY YOUTH,
AND FOR YOUR FORMER SHAME I SHALL
YOU GIVE YOU A DOUBLE RECOMPENSE AS
MY SON OR DAUGHTER.

HE MAKES **EVERYTHING** BEAUTIFUL IN ITS TIME

Ecclesiastes 3:1-15 (KJV)

¹ To everything there is a season, and a time to every purpose under the Heaven:
² A time to be born, and a time to die; a time to plant, and a time to pluck up that which is planted;
³ A time to kill, and a time to heal; a time to break down, and a time to build up;
⁴ A time to weep, and a time to laugh; a time to mourn, and a time to dance;
⁵ A time to cast away stones, and a time to gather stones together; a time to embrace, and a time to refrain from embracing;
⁶ A time to get, and a time to lose; a time to keep, and a time to cast away;
⁷ A time to rend, and a time to sew; a time to keep silence, and a time to speak;
⁸ A time to love, and a time to hate; a time of war, and a time of peace.
⁹ What profit hath he that worketh in that wherein he laboureth?
¹⁰ I have seen the travail, which God hath given to the sons of men to be exercised in it.
¹¹ He hath made everything beautiful in His time: also He hath set the world in their heart, so that no man can find out the work that God maketh from the beginning to the end.
¹² I know that there is no good in them, but for a man to rejoice, and to do good in his life.
¹³ And also that every man should eat and drink, and enjoy the good of all his labour, it is the gift of God.
¹⁴ I know that, whatsoever God doeth, it shall be forever: nothing can be put to it, nor anything taken from it: and God doeth it, that men should fear before Him.
¹⁵ That which hath been is now; and that which is to be hath already been; and God requireth that which is past.

Chapter One

BROKEN DREAMS

Have you ever known people who seem to always be on top of the mountain no matter what? Even in the face of adversity, they bounce back. They are successful, overall happy, perhaps married with children, and appear to have that perfect life; or have you ever known people or groups of people that have something like a dark cloud that constantly looms over their life? Disaster, drama, stressful moments, daily emergencies, and frantic panic attacks are their way of life. We all may know people who live a joyfully blessed life, and others who always live under some kind of curse.

Have you ever known anyone who professes to be a Christian, but still has a certain death sentence hanging over them in a particular area of their life? Maybe they have an addiction, illness, pain, past wounds, regret, shame, broken relationships or failed marriages that has marked their life as failure. You may know someone that looks like all hope is gone, and they will never recover. Bouncing back just isn't an option for them, because they are so scarred with unquenchable pain, and every day to them is a battle of survival.

If you or someone you know is a hopeless case, a real mess, and it looks absolutely *impossible* for any kind of breakthrough, I want to encourage you to keep reading. I want you to make a decision right now that you are going to stay focused, and receive your miracle or help someone else receive theirs. As my story unfolds, you may find yourself in a similar place just like I was; without hope, having a heart shattered into so many tiny little pieces that it was beyond repair or recognition.

Our early years

It was December 17, 1986, I was fifteen years old, and Mike was seventeen. Mike and I had a little crush on each other for a while before he ever made his first move. I will never forget the moment. He came out to visit me at my old farmhouse where I grew up, and we managed to talk for a while upstairs privately away from my parents. We were both so young, but it was quite obvious we liked each other. I don't think either of us really wanted to admit our feelings. While sitting on the edge of my bed, we were looking deep into each other's eyes, and before I knew it, there it was! He lunged in, and with a real starry look in his eyes we had our first kiss.

My heart instantly melted. I had braces at the time, and it felt awkward at first, but it was exciting and new. That's all it took, then I was hooked. Mike and I dated over a period of six years. We were engaged three times; once when I was seventeen, then nineteen, and finally, again at age twenty-one.

We had a truly unique relationship. We were high school sweethearts. We loved the same music, and had so much in common. When we were together we were inseparable, and the best of friends. We also were rebels, lone rangers, fighters and brawlers. Sometimes we acted so foolish, and jealousy filled us with rage. We were the most rebellious kids around. I am not at all proud of those things from our past, but that was who we were back then growing up.

Mike always knew exactly how to touch my heart. I was *extremely* melancholy with a very serious type personality. Somehow, he always managed to make me laugh, and understood me in ways that no one else could. We would go for motorcycle and car rides, and I remember feeling so free and alive when we were together.

For his eighteenth birthday, I got all dolled up, and baked him a chocolate birthday cake. It was the first cake I had ever baked. I am not sure why this happened, but it came out on a slope. It was a lopsided chocolate on chocolate cake, but he loved it! It was his special day, and I wanted him to feel so loved and adored. I always made a great big deal about his birthday. I was so glad that he had been born. He deserved to know how special he was to me, and that was just one way of showing him my love and adoration. We were like two peas in a pod.

As time moved on, he decided he was going to go into the Marine Corps after graduating high school. I was devastated by this decision. He was my life. He was everything to me, and I needed him. I couldn't understand why he had to leave. I remember going to the federal building, and saying our last goodbyes. I was so brokenhearted. Life was quickly taking a major downward turn, and I felt totally helpless. Why would he choose to leave me behind? How could he do this to me? Questions like these began flooding my mind. Over and over, I would play and replay hurtful episodes through my mind. My mind became a terrible frantic mess. I became deeply depressed beyond words. I was already so serious by nature. Add to that the depression of losing my best friend, and leaning on alcohol as a temporary relief, I learned to exist, and tried to cope by hiding the pain.

We spent the next few years in a very long distance relationship barely surviving on love letters, too many to recount. We would talk on the telephone as often as he could call, but it was never enough, and always went by so fast. My heart was torn up continually. I could never forgive him for leaving me. The pain in my heart was so overwhelming. My life as a young girl was being shaped for disaster, and I didn't even know it.

We grew up in a private Baptist school where all but a slim handful of people were used against us. People were always gossiping, pointing fingers, judging and criticizing our relationship, and trying their level best to break us up. I would hear all the benefits of breaking up playing and replaying in my mind. People were so good at giving me their unsolicited opinions. It was such a confusing part of my life.

Here I was, raised in this Baptist church where on one hand, I would hear sermons and what they believed, but then was surrounded by people whose lives contradicted the very thing that was being preached. Maybe you can relate. People would flat out tell lies to me or to Mike about me, and unfortunately we were both so jealous, crazy jealous, that the devil had gotten full control of our relationship. Those lies were continuously feeding tormenting spirits that harassed us with deception. At every turn, the devil was there making sure he would use what appeared to be "good intentioned" people to break us up.

There were several people in particular who were used by Satan commonly, and on a very regular basis. They would stir up trouble, try to cause doubt about our love for each other, and destroy our commitment to one another. Some of these people the devil used to destroy our love were some of our closest friends. Others were no doubt our biggest enemies, who were wolves in sheep's clothing. Because we were both insanely jealous and insecure at times, the devil would be sure to launch every fiery dart he had in his arsenal to hold us captive in bondage.

Our relationship became one big smoke screen filled with fear, hate, rage, anger, insecurity and jealousy. Neither one of us knew how to communicate our feelings of love for one another properly. Speaking the truth in love was not something we had been taught, so there wasn't ever any of that! Our suspicions grew toward each other, even though our love for one another was so strong and evident when we were together without interference. We had absolutely no power in our lives at that time to recognize the devil's tactics, nor did we understand who we were in Christ. All these things combined were probably some of the biggest tragedies we experienced in our childhood.

Both raised in Christian homes, a Christian church, and a Christian school, one may assume we should have been smarter than the devil, but that wasn't the case back then. We were blind, and living in darkness, and didn't even know it.

The devil knew that it had been written in the Bible that God had a good plan for our lives. The devil knew long before we ever did that God had a plan for us: Mike and Rhonda. The devil knew that if he could keep us living in sin and darkness, that it would almost be impossible for our love to ever endure any kind of hardship.

Eventually, Mike and I would have arguments on a regular basis; we'd temporarily break up, and then be right back together. We would go out with other people knowing it would hurt one another, but we did it anyway. Destruction and trouble seemed to follow us everywhere. He finally got out of the Marine Corps in the fall of 1992. We were on again, off again, time and time again.

There was one person in particular that Mike had gone out with that used to really make me mad. Even if I was upset with him, in my ignorance as a young girl, I still didn't want him going out with anyone else. The person he went out with was constantly telling lies about her and Mike's relationship, but I didn't know any better. I just believed what I heard from her. She was used by Satan to utterly destroy our relationship and trust. She was the tool that the enemy would use to chip away at us, little by little. It was a perpetual problem. This girl would sometimes come into my workplace and taunt me. She would make false accusations, and flaunt the fact that Mike had dumped me for her. I mentioned earlier that Mike and I were engaged three times. Every single time that we would argue, it looked like he was cheating on me with her or running back to her every time we were apart. It seemed at that time he was choosing her over me, at least that is what I believed back then. With everything I heard from her, coupled with Mike not being able to communicate his feelings very well, this left us both brokenhearted in the end. Finally, I had enough. As a result, I applied for a transfer out of state with my job, and relocated to Florida in June 1993.

I am with you. I have promised you that I will never leave you, nor forsake you. It seems now that your life is over. I am here with you. You can't feel or see Me right now. For I have hidden Myself from your senses, but I am alive in your heart. You have much to learn that will not be wasted. For the life lessons I am granting you shall not be for nothing. No, I have a specific purpose in everything. That the glory of My splendor shall be seen in greater measures, you will be permitted to suffer, but just for a little while. The pain you are experiencing is real. It's because you live in a world where demons and Satan rule over men. Many of My people have been taken captive at Satan's will. I am the great I AM. No one can ever pluck you out of My hand. For I have redeemed you from the hand of the enemy. I am fighting for you. I am with you. My eyes are upon you, My child.

Chapter Two

SHATTERED LIVES

The decision was made; I needed to move on with my life as difficult as it was. I contacted Mike, and told him I needed to see him. We stood in his parent's driveway as I explained to him that I was transferring with my job, and moving to Florida. I was saying my last goodbye, and told him not to try to stop me. My mind had been made up. I had reached the point of no return. Pain and countless tears in my hometown was all I knew. I was so ready to move far away to get a brand new start. I felt so depressed, rejected and unloved. Even though I was the one moving away, I felt like he had abandoned me. After all, had he not of left for the Marine Corps, then none of this would have happened, and there wouldn't have been any curse of separation between us.

For many years I suffered with the painful "what if" scenarios over and over in my mind. You know what I mean, the "what if" things would have been different thoughts. He was the only man I had ever truly loved. He was my first love; he was my one and only. All the memories I had with Mike I would try to soon forget and move on. I wanted to erase all the pain from our past to make it null and void. My mind wasn't able to bury the painful memories very long. It just wasn't easy. That was a never ending process. No matter how hard I would try to forget about him, it was impossible.

For a very long time, in fact years, I was so angry toward him. We had once been the best of friends, but sadly bitterness and resentment followed me around for many long dreadful years. People I would meet or date would ask me about myself. I would tell people how I dated this guy over a period of six years; that we were engaged three times, but then always finished my sad story with how he cheated on me, and couldn't be trusted anymore. For over twenty years, even until Christmas 2014, I still spoke of Mike as the one guy I only ever truly loved who broke my heart continuously.

It really damages a person to hold on to past memories of pain. I loved him so deeply, but felt like I would never be able to trust him or anyone else for that matter ever again.

After I moved to Florida, I had a very difficult time in relationships. With numerous valid reasons, I trusted no one. What I am about to share used to be true for me. Before you read on, please be assured I do not feel this way today. Until Jesus Christ healed my broken heart and shattered soul, I had a very bad outlook on life, especially toward relationships. I have had to renew my mind to the Word of God, and allow His love to dominate my thinking and my life.

Based on past history and experience, almost every person I had a relationship with gave me concrete proof to my theory that all men were liars, cheaters or pigs. Again, please understand that I do not feel this way today, but those tainted thoughts while living in darkness, combined with a negative outlook on life didn't happen overnight. With God's help, He has taught me it's a learning process over time to trust Him to change me. As I do my part to renew my mind in accordance to His Word, He has shown me how to walk in forgiveness. In doing so, I have been able to let go of bitterness and resentment for the injustices and wrongs I have endured.

At different seasons in my life, the devil set traps for all kinds of crazy guys to find me, and relentlessly hunt me down; some were stalkers, and many forms of abuse, manipulation, and deception were used to get me to stay in a relationship with them. In some other fewer cases, I was abandoned. God's hand was never in any of those destructive relationships to begin with. *The devil is methodically seductive and deceptive.*

Over the years, I would be in one bad relationship, and then another. After many years of torment, one by one I had to learn to forgive. Yes, it was quite a battle for me to forgive. The abusive pain I suffered was on *every* level including physical, mental, and emotional through some of these problematic relationships.

The devil's plan was to derail me all along. He wanted to take me out. The Bible says that Satan is our adversary, who roams about like a roaring lion seeking whom he may devour (First Peter 5:8). I have forgiven all those who have hurt me from my past. Eventually, I got around to even forgiving myself, which was one of the hardest battles I have ever faced. It's not because I had any ability to forgive, and let go in and of myself. I will share with you a practical way that has helped me to get free from past or present pain.

Past failures, former shame, roots of bitterness, resentment, and rage seemed to be a way of life for me. Going from one bad relationship to the next, I never really took the time needed to search my own heart, repent for my mistakes, and allow God's love to heal my wounds. One of my greatest desires was to stop repeating the same mistakes, but apart from God's help, I didn't know how to do this on my own. I honestly didn't know anything about healthy relationships, how to trust a man or even simply how to be happy. For over twenty plus years of my adult life, I didn't even like myself. I hated my life. Feelings of sorrow and inadequate self-consciousness surrounded me like a dark gloomy cloud. People couldn't be trusted, relationships hurt, people were liars and undependable; that was all I knew or thought.

As I look back now, it's so much easier to see why God allowed me to go through such painful and hurtful situations. I now can sympathize and understand why people who have experienced devastating events are sometimes filled with spirits of fear, rage and bitterness. Many have an inability to forgive, and live under extreme torment. Many of us battle strife, contention, rejection and defeat. Today, through the ministry of the Holy Spirit showing me God's love, mercy and grace, I have learned how to be free from those yokes of bondage.

Every major decision I made after Mike and I broke up was based upon what I realized much later in life was all a lie. *It was a powerful lie that I had believed for twenty-one and a half years, which altered my life completely.* This is one reason why I am so passionate about sharing my story. I am striving to spark a hope in you to ignite a fire that will change your course from what may be destructive, into a brand new life of passion and purpose. It's possible, but it's only possible with a relationship with Father God, through His Son Jesus Christ, and the work and ministry of the Holy Spirit. The Holy Spirit will lead and guide us into all truth when we walk before Him with our whole heart.

1 Peter 1:6-8 (KJV)

⁶ Wherein ye greatly rejoice, though now for a season, if need be, ye are in heaviness through manifold temptations:

⁷ That the trial of your faith, being much more precious than of gold that perisheth, though it be tried with fire, might be found unto praise and honour and glory at the appearing of Jesus Christ:

⁸ Whom having not seen, ye love; in whom, though now ye see Him not, yet believing, ye rejoice with joy unspeakable and full of glory.

Psalm 127:1a (KJV)

Except the LORD build the house, they labour in vain that build it.

Get moving in the right direction

Father God, I pray that You will give me the ability and strength needed to forgive all those who have hurt or betrayed me, all those who have ever spoken lies to or about me, and all those who have violated me. Please heal my broken heart now. Let me feel the embrace of Your love wrapped all around me. By faith today, I release and forgive all those who have sinned against me.

I believe that the sacrifice Jesus made on the cross was enough for the sins of all people. I pray that You would pour out Your love, mercy, and forgiveness upon those who have hurt me. I trust You to bind up all the wounds of my broken heart with Your healing oil. Please forgive me for all known and unknown sins I have committed. By faith, I also forgive myself, and let go of all my shame now, and receive Your love, mercy, and grace in the mighty Name of Jesus. Amen!

If you just prayed that prayer earnestly from the depths of your heart, you have been forgiven, and can rest now; knowing that God will move on your behalf to make all those wrongs right. Be bold, take a risk, go out on the skinny branch, and trust Him today.

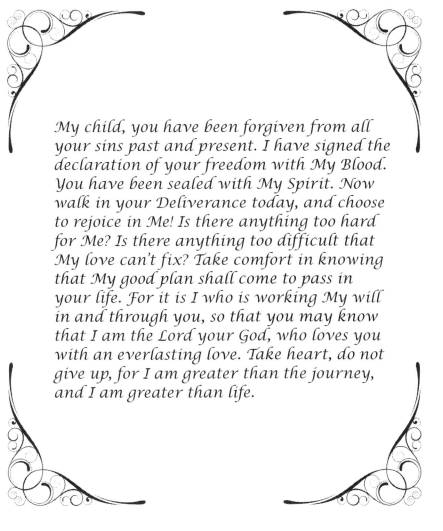

My child, you have been forgiven from all your sins past and present. I have signed the declaration of your freedom with My Blood. You have been sealed with My Spirit. Now walk in your Deliverance today, and choose to rejoice in Me! Is there anything too hard for Me? Is there anything too difficult that My love can't fix? Take comfort in knowing that My good plan shall come to pass in your life. For it is I who is working My will in and through you, so that you may know that I am the Lord your God, who loves you with an everlasting love. Take heart, do not give up, for I am greater than the journey, and I am greater than life.

Chapter Three

BOUND, BLIND, BRUISED, BEATEN AND BROKEN

Walking in newness of life brings forth the revelation and knowledge of God in His Light. The new life from above helps us to overcome the challenges and battles we face daily.

We can overcome fear, doubt, and all the lies of the devil. The enemy's tactics are made known to us as we spend time in God's Word and His presence, and then He begins to reveal those hidden treasures of truth to us by the Holy Spirit. We stay on His path of righteousness as we seek His face, and listen for His voice to guide our steps. He delivers us out of the snare of the enemy, out of the enemy's trap for our good, and to His glory and praise.

Believing lies and deceit causes continual despair and defeat.

God wants to use me as a broken vessel that has been healed and made whole for His glory, and to His praise, so I share with you my true story. May the eyes of your heart be opened now as my story unfolds, to give you hope for a much brighter and happier future.

He also wants us to help others out of their darkness so that they, too, can walk in the freedom of the light of the glorious Gospel.

We must be willing to allow Him to teach us lessons through life's experiences based upon His Word.

Maybe you've heard about spiritual warfare. Perhaps you are very familiar with it, while others may not be. Either way, we are all doing battle every day against our flesh, the world and the devil. Every day is a spiritual battle. *We can either take charge over these areas that affect our lives or do nothing, and they will master us!*

There are a few Bible passages that I want to share with you, and show you a direct correlation from their story to mine. I believe this is important, and may help shed some light in your own life to help get you free from some of the areas that you've been battling for a very long time.

Luke 13: 11-16 (KJV)

[11] And, behold, there was a woman which had a spirit of infirmity eighteen years, and was bowed together, and could in no wise lift up herself.

[12] And when Jesus saw her, He called her to Him, and said unto her, "Woman, thou art loosed from thine infirmity."

[13] And He laid His hands on her: and immediately she was made straight, and glorified God.

[14] And the ruler of the synagogue answered with indignation, because that Jesus had healed on the Sabbath day, and said unto the people, "There are six days in which men ought to work: in them therefore come and be healed, and not on the Sabbath day."

[15] The Lord then answered him, and said, "Thou hypocrite, doth not each one of you on the Sabbath loose his ox or his ass from the stall, and lead him away to watering?

¹⁶ *And ought not this woman, being a daughter of Abraham, whom Satan hath bound, lo, these eighteen years, be loosed from this bond on the Sabbath day?"*

Mark 10:46-52 (KJV)

⁴⁶ *And they came to Jericho: and as He went out of Jericho with His disciples and a great number of people, blind Bartimaeus, the son of Timaeus, sat by the highway side begging.*

⁴⁷ *And when he heard that it was Jesus of Nazareth, he began to cry out, and say, "Jesus, thou son of David, have mercy on me."*

⁴⁸ *And many charged him that he should hold his peace: but he cried the more a great deal, "Thou son of David, have mercy on me."*

⁴⁹ *And Jesus stood still, and commanded him to be called. And they called the blind man, saying unto him, "Be of good comfort, rise; He calleth thee."*

⁵⁰ *And he, casting away his garment, rose, and came to Jesus.*

⁵¹ *And Jesus answered and said unto him, "What wilt thou that I should do unto thee?" The blind man said unto him, "Lord, that I might receive my sight."*

⁵² *And Jesus said unto him, "Go thy way; thy faith hath made thee whole." And immediately he received his sight, and followed Jesus in the way.*

Mark 5:25-34 (KJV)

²⁵ *And a certain woman, which had an issue of blood twelve years,*

²⁶ *And had suffered many things of many physicians, and had spent all that she had, and was nothing bettered, but rather grew worse,*

²⁷ *When she had heard of Jesus, came in the press behind, and touched His garment.*

28 For she said, "If I may touch but His clothes, I shall be whole."

29 And straightway the fountain of her blood was dried up; and she felt in her body that she was healed of that plague.

30 And Jesus, immediately knowing in Himself that virtue had gone out of Him, turned Him about in the press, and said, "Who touched my clothes?"

31 And His disciples said unto Him, "Thou seest the multitude thronging Thee, and sayest thou, 'Who touched me'?"

32 And He looked round about to see her that had done this thing.

33 But the woman fearing and trembling, knowing what was done in her, came and fell down before Him, and told Him all the truth.

34 And He said unto her, "Daughter, thy faith hath made thee whole; go in peace, and be whole of thy plague."

According to Galatians 3:13, we have been redeemed from the curse of the Law. God's wrath was poured out upon His Son in our stead. Jesus took our place, and the punishment we deserved. Those who believe on the Name of Jesus through salvation's experience are free from that awful curse of the Law, because He became a curse for us.

Now notice in Luke 13:16 who it was that had bound this woman; it was the devil. You see, the god (Satan) of this world has full reign over the world system (see Second Corinthians 4:4). Satan, the enemy of our soul, absolutely loves to put sickness, disease, and poverty upon all people; he causes suffering everywhere around the world, but in Acts 10:38 we see how *"Jesus went about doing good, and healing all those who were oppressed by the devil."* We know by the Word of God that Jesus was manifested to destroy all, not some, of the works of the devil.

Galatians 3:13-16, 26-29 (KJV)

¹³ Christ hath redeemed us from the curse of the law, being made a curse for us: for it is written, "Cursed is every one that hangeth on a tree:"

¹⁴ That the blessing of Abraham might come on the Gentiles through Jesus Christ; that we might receive the promise of the Spirit through faith.

¹⁵ Brethren, I speak after the manner of men; Though it be but a man's covenant, yet if it be confirmed, no man disannulleth, or addeth thereto.

¹⁶ Now to Abraham and his seed were the promises made. He saith not, and to seeds, as of many; but as of one, and to thy seed, which is Christ.

²⁶ For ye are all the children of God by faith in Christ Jesus.

²⁷ For as many of you as have been baptized into Christ have put on Christ.

²⁸ There is neither Jew nor Greek, there is neither bond nor free, there is neither male nor female: for ye are all one in Christ Jesus.

²⁹ And if ye be Christ's, then are ye Abraham's seed, and heirs according to the promise.

Did you know that Jesus not only came to seek and save those who were lost, but He also went about doing God's will which includes healing the brokenhearted? Jesus came to destroy all the works of our adversary, the devil. The woman who was bound for eighteen years probably felt hopeless and worthless, and she may have been called many unfavorable names.

One thing that I have learned is sometimes our pain inadvertently becomes our identity. I know for me it did. As a matter of fact, sometimes I think pain likes to try to make its home with us. If we don't ever take a risk, and enter into the presence of the Lord, we may never know how miraculous His wonder-working power really is! *You see, she put herself in a position to get noticed by the Master, Christ the Healer.* While her heart isn't exposed, and we don't know much about her spiritual life, we do know that she somehow managed to get herself into an atmosphere where her healing took place, and she got her miracle! Notice in the scripture above that she was a daughter of Abraham, which means she had privileges and rights as a covenant child of God.

Why then did she have to suffer those eighteen long years? We do not know all the reasons. We only know in part, and the secret things belong unto the Lord. The parts that are revealed belong to us. What we don't know or can't figure out must be surrendered unto the Lord in trust. *Trusting Him in those hard to face places of our lives may not always be easy. I can tell you though through experience, God always makes His word good.*

According to the New Testament, if you are a Gentile like me, we are grafted into the Vine, which is Jesus Christ. When it comes to God's love and freedom, the kind of freedom we experience through our relationship with the Father through Jesus Christ, the Lord sees no difference between male or female, Jew nor Greek, because He is no respecter of persons. If you belong to Jesus Christ, and are a child of the Most High God, then you as a believer have a legal right to be free as sons and daughters of Abraham.

Blind Bartimaeus was able to perceive something without his natural sight. Do you know what he perceived? I believe he perceived there was a Healer in town. He also must have been convinced that Jesus was indeed the son of David, and had believed that Jesus was a man of compassion. How do we know this? Because Blind Bartimaeus said, "Son of David have mercy on me." He was willing to take a step of faith, and discard his old garment when he was told that Jesus was calling for him. That old garment signifying blindness was his previous identification before he received his miracle. *He humbly cried out for help, and help came to his rescue.*

The woman with the issue of blood had to press past a whole lot of hurt before she received her miracle healing. This woman had nothing and nobody on her side cheering her on. She was faced with a choice. Press past the physical, mental and emotional pain to get to the One she knew would heal or stay stuck in her pain. Her identity may have been one that you and I could relate. One being rejected, who lost all her money, and had lived with the same battle for twelve years; her mind was probably in horrendous torment. I suspect her emotions were severely wounded and bruised; her worth and value were probably beaten so far down that she may have wondered if anyone even cared that she was alive. That woman's heart to say the least must have been broken. *In the natural, her situation may have looked impossible, but it's only people who are in need of a miracle get one!*

What I've learned from these three true biblical accounts are major life lessons. For decades I was bound by the devil, under severe attack, and hopelessly depressed. Days without number I was blind. I couldn't detect a counterfeit love from the genuine. I was so easily deceived. If that's not enough, I also believed and was convinced about something that was a life altering lie for twenty-one and a half years. Because of something bad that happened way back there in my past, my present and future were always hijacked. My emotions and feelings were perpetually bruised, causing me to be extremely touchy, angry, resentful and fretful. Many people's words spoken over my life had me so far beaten down at times, that I had no real self-confidence, self-esteem or value. For years and years, my heart was empty, void of love and completely broken.

There's so much to take away from these real life biblical accounts we just read about. What I want you to see now is that sometimes, in order for God to move on your behalf and do something miraculous for you, *it may take some work on your part*. Sometimes, you may need to get out of your wrong thinking patterns. You might need to get away from religious folks who say things like, "Miracles used to happen back in the Bible days, but it's not for today." Perhaps you need to swim upstream, and not go with the flow. You may need to humble yourself, and acknowledge the Lord Jesus Christ as your Healer, and not your medicine. Medicine can and some doctors may help you progress along the way, that's true; but miracles with or without medication do really happen. Most of all, God wants you to believe in Him to perform on your behalf.

I want you to be encouraged and inspired, because dreams can really become your reality. Ask God to help you. Seek the truth, knock, and keep on knocking for your breakthrough, and then only believe!

Isaiah 10:27 (KJV)

And it shall come to pass in that day, that his burden shall be taken away from off thy shoulder, and his yoke from off thy neck, and the yoke shall be destroyed because of the anointing.

Matthew 7:7 (KJV)

Ask, and it shall be given you; seek, and ye shall find; knock, and it shall be opened unto you.

Mark 9:23 (KJV)

Jesus said unto him, "If thou canst believe, all things are possible to him that believeth."

Only believe.

Only believe.

There's just one thing I desire from you right now.

Only believe.

Believe in Me, believe on Me. Believe I am the Christ that healeth thee.

Believe on Me, lean on Me. Only believe, and you will see all things I have promised you shall come to pass.

Only believe!

Chapter Four

HOODWINKED

Throughout my entire life, Satan was sure to use people as bait to lure me further and further away from the truth of knowing who I was in Christ. In the book of Romans chapter twelve, we are exhorted to offer up our bodies as a living sacrifice unto the Lord. I used to live like the world. I dressed like and behaved as the world does. There wasn't much outward difference between anyone without Christ in their life or mine.

Even as a believer of Jesus Christ for many long years, I hadn't yet really received the valuable revelation that our bodies are indeed the temple of the Holy Spirit. Inside our fleshly body, where our spirit man dwells, is where the fullness of Almighty God our Creator lives. Once I received that deep truth into my heart, my life began to take on a new identity in Christ. I used to blame people for a lot of the havoc that the devil was bringing into my life. Satan, the enemy of our soul, does everything possible to get us to point our fingers at others, while not accepting responsibility for our own willful actions. I say willful, because I also know what it's like being violated against my own will.

It's so vitally important to understand that sometimes people are used as vessels that the enemy can flow through. I love all people; Jesus commands us to love all people, but I sure don't like what sin does to a person or how it makes one behave. Satan is my enemy, not people, but the devil had me on "play and repeat." He would push play repeatedly, and I would choose unwisely again and again. Over and over, the enemy of my soul would use men to violate my temple, my mind, emotions, heart and body; either by my own consent through deception or by their own force against my will.

It was common ground for me to be identified by my past mistakes and failures. Maybe you or someone you know has experienced something similar. I would always try to do better, and not make the same mistakes, not realizing back then apart from God, and without a strong vibrant relationship with Jesus Christ, I alone couldn't help my situations or circumstances. I couldn't break free from the vicious cycle of bad relationships I was once held captive to.

During those seemingly hopeless seasons in my life, I was given labels to wear by well meaning, "good intentioned" religious folks, who made it their mission to judge and criticize me. Some of the people would attempt to explain to me why I had such horrible relationships, and then tried to "fix" me. Although they never walked in my shoes, somehow they thought they were above me, more sophisticated or spiritual than me, but in reality many times people were really looking down their nose at me. People's constant judgment and criticism made me want to avoid them, even though I loved many who tried to help.

The pattern of my life was shaped by constant defeat, followed by those who judged in their hearts against me, and then would gossip about my situations. This in turn created major despair in my world. I was always in a constant state of hopelessness. It was rare to find anyone that I could really trust with my feelings, or share private details of my life to get answers to help me. My life was full of darkness, having no hope for any kind of future, and I had especially given up on marriage. There was an inability on my part to induce any positive change in my life. Opinionated judgments coupled with constant criticism bombarded my soul. *Satan loves to use people as fiery darts to weaken our hearts, and keep us paralyzed in pain.*

The demons sent to destroy my life knew no end to their torments. The devil can keep us in bondage as long as he can convince us that we are a "nobody" and a "nothing." No one in their right mind wants or desires to be a slave to anyone. We all instinctively know that's wrong, but sometimes we can be bound to sinful man, our flesh, the world, or the devil, and sometimes not even be aware of it.

The devil used to love making me think that it was okay to hate people for their wrongdoing, and kept me in a prison of hatred for many years. Since that time, I have now learned that we do not wrestle against flesh and blood, but as stated before, we definitely are in a battle! It's a spiritual battle for our very souls. I had been in an unseen war with devils, demons, high and low ranking principalities, and even Satan himself. Until I learned the truth about "who I am in Christ," and began getting rooted and grounded in God's Word and His amazing love, I was an easy target for Satan. Today, we all are in a spiritual war, and need to be equipped with truth, love, faith, hope, a tenacious spirit, and power from the Holy Spirit in order to win the battles we face daily.

Until we know the truth of every matter we will always be held captive in some sort of bondage. Jesus spoke in John chapter eight about how we need to invest our time to get to know *The Truth,* and allow His truth to settle in our hearts. He made a promise, and He always keeps His promises. The essence of what I've learned through that passage is that He said if we would continue in His Word, we would know the truth (or in other words, I should endeavor to seek truth out for myself, have my own walk and relationship with Him) then the power of knowing and having that knowledge of His truth, and *acting upon it* would make us free.

One of the greatest pleasures for the devil was keeping me as his pet puppet. He was a master at tormenting my soul, and would get me to yield and fall right into his traps of deception. His tormenting tactics and mind-game schemes started early in my life from childhood.

Remember this: The truth about any matter will always be settled by the Word of God.

Seasons change, reports change, people change, circumstances change, but the Word of God never changes. *The grass withereth, the flower fadeth: but the word of our God shall stand forever (Isaiah 40:8 KJV).* The Word of God never lies, and can only speak truth. That truth must be rightly divided, and not used out of context. When the truth is spoken it must be with a conviction of agape love, God's love. Man's love is fickle and can change, but thank God, the Word declares, *"Jesus Christ, the same yesterday, today and forever"* (Hebrews 13:8). Hallelujah!

I'm so thankful, because I am seeing more and more how God really does honor His Word in my life. Life's circumstances of being misjudged, misunderstood, abused or used by the devil is absolutely no match for a person who consistently seeks after God with their whole heart. Eventually, the truth of every matter will be resolved. Payday comes, and the Lord has proven in my life, He is capable of turning what was evil and vile around for my good, and to His glory.

God, the One true living God is a God of justice. He is always good; always seeking to do good for us, and is always faithful to His Word and His Bride. He honors those who love mercy, and purposefully live to bring Him glory; those who act justly, and walk humbly before their God.

Micah 6:8 (KJV)

He hath shewed thee, O man, what is good; and what doth the LORD require of thee, but to do justly, and to love mercy, and to walk humbly with thy God?

Romans 8:26-32 (KJV)

²⁶ Likewise the Spirit also helpeth our infirmities: for we know not what we should pray for as we ought: but the Spirit itself [Himself] maketh intercession for us with groanings which cannot be uttered.

²⁷ And He that searcheth the hearts knoweth what is the mind of the Spirit, because He maketh intercession for the saints according to the will of God.

²⁸ And we know that all things work together for good to them that love God, to them who are the called according to His purpose.

²⁹ For whom He did foreknow, He also did predestinate to be conformed to the image of His Son, that He might be the firstborn among many brethren.

³⁰ Moreover whom He did predestinate, them He also called: and whom He called, them He also justified: and whom He justified, them He also glorified.

³¹ What shall we then say to these things? If God be for us, who can be against us?

³² He that spared not His own Son, but delivered Him up for us all, how shall He not with Him also freely give us all things?

1 Samuel 2:30 (KJV)

*Wherefore the L*ORD *God of Israel saith, "I said indeed that thy house, and the house of thy father, should walk before me forever:" but now the L*ORD *saith, "Be it far from me; for them that honour me I will honour, and they that despise me shall be lightly esteemed."*

The Truth of every matter is settled by My Word.

I will help you see Truth so that you will not be deceived.

You are Mine, you belong to Me. Abide in My Word, and practice doing My Word. Allow My Word to penetrate your spirit and your soul. Revelation by My Spirit shall be poured out upon you. You shall know the Truth, and My Truth will make you free.

Chapter Five

FINAL ANALYSIS

In the final analysis, opposition proved dominant over my life. For many years I carried around with me a broken soul, one of painful rejection, which in turn fed a spirit of despair. That spirit of despair grew larger and larger over time, and finally birthed a passive spirit, enabling me to compromise or settle, even when I knew better!

Do you understand what it means to settle? Sometimes through my pain I went ahead and settled, thinking at the moment maybe that was really my lot in life; to feel depressed and be unhappy, and that was just as good as it could get. Maybe you've been there before, or if not you, maybe someone you know settles. I wanted to believe that there were good people out there. Every time I saw a tiny glimmer of hope and would grasp for it, the enemy would always set a trap to keep me buried in hopelessness; followed by reckless decisions, which invoked severe consequences, and ultimately, I landed in a pit of despair and darkness.

I can remember about eight years ago, I was spending Christmas with some special friends of mine. I was amongst two strong Christian couples that were at that time the only people I felt I could open up to, and get good godly advice from. These were friends I valued and trusted.

One from the group posed a question, and asked us to share what our favorite Christmas memory was as a child. That question led to another topic; I was then asked what I was looking for in a relationship since I was single. At that time, that was a pretty easy question for me to respond to. For some time, I had been praying and believing God, that one day He would grant me the desires of my heart.

My confession for a long time had been that my life was so hidden in Christ, that my husband would have to seek God first with his whole heart, and then he would find me there in the presence of Almighty God. With all sincerity and hopefulness, I answered the question, and said that I had asked the Lord to give me a husband, a real husband who would love God more than me, and love me second only to Him. I continued, and said that I had also requested from the Lord that this future husband not have any deceit found in his heart or in his lips. Immediately, the atmosphere changed, and I knew I made a really big mistake by sharing my dreams.

This may have seemed like an impossible request to them, I know, but I really thought that I could ask God for something I desired and maybe, just maybe, one day my dream of this hard to find man would come true for me. Almost everyone in the room busted out laughing at what they perceived as my ridiculous request. I was told that what I was believing God for was *impossible!* They did everything to convince me that it was no use at all to believe for such a ludicrous thing. I so badly just wanted to be loved; not taken advantage of, not lied to, not abused, or cheated on. *Don't ever let anyone tell you to stop believing for or dreaming about God's good plan for your life!*

As a direct result of my bad choices and compromise, failure and regret followed me everywhere. Now, please understand, from the time I was a little girl, I was taught that God hates divorce, and that divorce is wrong; even if people have problems, no matter what they are, divorce is *NEVER* the answer. That's what I grew up thinking, because that is exactly what I was taught. That was the general consensus of what most of my church friends and some family members believed, too. I heard the same kind of things many times over from various pulpits.

Despite what I had been taught growing up, I had fallen into all kinds of traps of abusive relationships over the years. The impact of my poorly repeated choices changed the very course of my life; it grew steadily from bad to worse. I absolutely had lost all hope of ever being able to trust anyone again. I had gotten to the point of not ever wanting to even date again. Dating was the most dangerous affair, because that's where all the "crazy" always began for me in every instance.

Confusion ran rampant in my life when people were excessively angry or abusive toward me, and I was unsure how to respond. It was confusing, because I would want to be patient and loving toward people, while they needed help or deliverance; but then on the other hand, I would wonder if it was wrong for me to protect myself from harm's way. It was a constant state of chaos many times, not knowing if I was supposed to just tolerate misbehavior, or what the right thing was to do. Not knowing what to do in those hard times kept me in bondage, not knowing if I was supposed to put up with it, or get out *(and still be practicing my love walk)*. I didn't know how to enforce proper boundaries, and people would manipulate or put huge guilt-trips on me, so life many times was a constant battle, filled with unnecessary drama. Torment and defeat were two things I had become most familiar with.

I understand what it's like to be abandoned, rejected and abused. I know what it's like to have to visit a women's shelter to try to get a grip on life; mine just seemed to be falling apart. The devil works overtime in a believer's life to keep him paralyzed, hindered, slowed down or knocked off track from God's divine plans and purposes. Satan's number one goal is to steal, kill, and destroy everything or anything that is valuable to one's life. If Satan is unsuccessful in stealing your salvation, then it's guaranteed he will work relentlessly to try to steal the abundant life Jesus wants you and I to have here on this earth.

Part of that abundant life that I was hoping to get one day was a man who truly loved me, who wouldn't abandon or abuse me, and could keep a promise to be faithful. Jesus loves us; He came to earth, made Himself of no reputation, selflessly died, and paid for all mankind's sin. He desires us to be in healthy, loving relationships, not ones filled with torment and pain.

When you get a revelation of the true nature and love of God, you can begin to see what it means in the Bible when it talks about a godly marriage. The husband is to love his wife just as Christ Jesus loves His Bride, the Church. The Word of God tells us that Jesus willingly laid down His own life as a sacrifice, and He came that we might have and enjoy our life in this lifetime (see John 10:10). Jesus also came to destroy all the works of the enemy, not just some. Likewise, a husband is commanded to love his wife. A part of that entails a sacrificial heart, a man who can lean on and trust in God, and love his bride unconditionally.

One thing that's needed most from men today to have a strong and healthy marriage, is for them to learn *how to love* their wives, lay down their flesh, take up their cross, and live on purpose like they've accepted Jesus as their Lord and Savior. They can then take their wife by the hand, and lead her in every situation to the One and only true God. It's so much easier for a woman to respect her husband as commanded by the Lord, when he is doing everything he can to please God, and not his flesh. Women desire to adapt to a man who loves them, who can provide them with security, and find ways to convey that they are the most beautiful, treasured woman in the world to him. Who wouldn't want that?

In no way do I claim to be an expert on any topic, especially relationships. Simply, I'm stating principles of truth about how God says a marriage or relationships should be. Jesus Christ is the only Answer for all of humanity. He is our only true source of joy, hope and strength. Apart from God, any man who tries to lead his wife knowingly or unknowingly away from Jesus Christ is doing more harm than good to his marriage. Only that which is done for Jesus Christ will hold an eternal value. I thank the Lord for sending His Holy Spirit to help lead and guide us into all truth. The Holy Spirit gives us power beyond our comprehension, and grace to help us in our times of struggle, pain or hardships.

A false reading

It isn't safe to trust in man or the arm of the flesh, including our own. I am not saying that there aren't any trustworthy men or women out there; please don't misunderstand. However, we are commanded to trust in the

Lord with all our heart, not man. The Lord, through the Word of God and by His Spirit, desires to be our source of strength and wisdom. Our first response in every situation should be to inquire of God, consult His Word, pray, and then believe that He is going to lead us to the right answers.

At times, God may speak to us through people. Just be aware that the devil can also speak to you through good, well-meaning, Spirit filled people, too! It's good sometimes to seek out godly counsel. Some potential hazards may be eliminated before they happen with good sound advice and counsel. Oftentimes though, some people we turn to and trust may be telling us something that contradicts what God has already promised us in His Word. He knows what's best for us, and that's why He wants us to seek after Him with our whole heart.

The Bible warns that people perish for lack of knowledge. Unless we seek out the truth for ourselves, and learn to rightly divide the Word of God, in some cases like mine, we can be easily led astray and deceived. My life was perishing for lack of knowledge of who I was in Christ, what privileges were mine as a child of the Most High God, and disobedience through ignorance or wrongful consent.

In the final analysis of my life, I had been married and divorced four times, and wasn't entertaining any thoughts of *EVER* being married again.

I do?

Listed here are some of the things that *all four* of my failed marriages had in common:

Not once was I given an engagement or a wedding ring, nor did I ever have a wedding gown, wedding accessories or jewelry. I actually picked out and paid for my first wedding ring. It was the only wedding ring I ever had, no other times in marriage was I ever given a "real" proposal, an engagement ring or even a wedding band. The ceremonies were never held in a church. Three of the four weddings were performed by either a notary or justice of the peace. No one during those four weddings ever gave me away. I never had a wedding cake or gifts to celebrate the new "Mr. and Mrs." at any of these weddings. There weren't ever any bridesmaids or maid of honor. There was never a wedding photographer at any of my weddings. I never lit any unity candle, nor performed any type of Holy Communion during any of these weddings. There was only a very small group of family at my first wedding, which occurred about five months after my dad had died. We all in my family were experiencing grief, and I was still extremely vulnerable over the loss of my dad at that time. I never considered my vows holy unto God or even cared to pray over my vows in any of those four marriages. As a matter of fact, I didn't even know ahead of time what the vows would be that would be read or spoken at any of my weddings. There wasn't ever any kind of planned wedding ceremony rehearsal, nor did I know the order of any of the process. There was never any honeymoon period, fun getaway or celebration for me as the new wife during any of these four marriages.

Looking back now, it makes me wonder if any of those works I permitted in the flesh apart from God could have ever brought any true blessings into my life. Yes, God can take anything from our past, including bad decisions we make, and somehow turn it around, and work it out for our good. Only because He is God and He is the only One capable of bringing us justice and redemption through the mighty power of His Holy Spirit. He can and does bring us true deliverance and love through Jesus Christ when we repent from our sins.

You see, God is a giver. He adds to our lives; He doesn't take away from us. We can see this principle all throughout the Bible over and over. His nature and character demonstrates that He is a giver (see John 3:16, Matthew 6:33, Jeremiah 33:3). We must call unto Him for wisdom, and search out His right way of doing things. He promises to give; He adds to, multiplies, and brings increase into our lives. Equally, He will not be mocked, and whatsoever we sow in this lifetime to the flesh (apart from God's initiation, plan, purposes or will) we can be sure we will reap corruption from the flesh (see Galatians 6:7-8). We can always count on enjoying peace, prosperity, and blessings when we are walking in the Spirit, even if all around us, we may at times see disasters or destruction. As long as we stay safe in the love of God and under His umbrella of protection, His blessings will flow to our lives. When I have gotten outside of His protection, and have done my own thing, I have learned that the consequences are severe.

Even in the example of the true account of Job in the Bible, it was Satan who stole from Job. Read the story! Some people quote Job and say, "The Lord gives, and the Lord takes away." I learned through Bible school that what Job said was recorded, and is reflected as being *truly stated* by Job. *It's what he said.* That is true, yes, but Job's statement he made was *NOT* a statement of truth! Job had no idea that Satan was the thief and destroyer; he thought God was the one doing Satan's dirty work. Yes, it's true that God permitted or gave permission to Satan to wreak havoc in Job's life, but look at the end of the story!

Job was blessed! He was absolutely blessed beyond measure, because he refused to stop serving God; even while it seemed his life was cursed, and he was walking out a sentence of death and destruction all around him. *Satan likes to take away our identity, steal our dignity, and most of all, he loves when people blame God as their source of pain and affliction.*

During my adult life, I had confessed to be a Christian, but it's obvious to me that I was not living the abundant life Jesus died to give me. I was not living in full obedience unto the Lord, which in turn I unknowingly opened many doors for the enemy to invade my life. I was living under a curse, many curses actually, for many years. If sharing my story helps you realize your enemy, the devil, is real, and that the power of the One true living God is *alive today,* then it's all worth it! God loves you, and is pursuing you, and wants you to come up higher in your walk with Him. It's His desire that we search His Holy Word for deep rich treasures that will bring prosperity into our lives.

The enemy is an expert at using people to lure us into his traps of deception. The people he is using to bring us defeat sometimes aren't even aware that they are being used by Satan to destroy us. Through wrong or sinful soul ties, wrong thinking or living outside of God's will and best for our lives, Satan can keep us bound up in continual bondage. These bondages may include stress, addictions, loneliness, anger, and many other countless, poisonous things he offers as his reward for indulgence to our flesh or the world. Satan always comes to bring confusion and destruction. He entices us with glamorous counterfeits! It's obvious to me now that none of the circumstances surrounding my former weddings were God's best for me.

As you may know, King David was known in the Bible as the man after God's own heart. Yet, in a moment, the enemy used beautiful Bathsheba to lure King David into temptation, whether she realized she was being used or not, that's the tool Satan used as a weapon against King David. King David's one sin of lust turned into adultery, and then murder. Thank God King David eventually repented, but as a direct result of his sin through deception, he suffered severe consequences.

I am absolutely no different than King David in that I am not immune to the devil's tricks or temptations. The devil had set up an enticing trap to ensnare King David. Satan does the same thing to all of us today; he knows exactly what our weak spots are, and then tries to create the "perfect opportunity" for us to be caught in his trap. The bait he uses may differ from one person to another, but his end goal is the same: Death and Destruction.

God's original plan

Are you familiar with the Old Testament account concerning King Saul? King Saul was made king over God's chosen people from man's fleshly choice. It was not God's choice for Israel to have an earthly king. He wanted to be their all in all, but they with hardened hearts wanted to do their own thing, and be like the world. There are always consequences for being outside of God's will for our lives.

We could examine the Scriptures in the Book of Genesis about Adam and Eve, and see how God's choice for Adam was to have one woman as his wife. God created Eve, and then took and introduced her to Adam. God knew exactly what was best for Adam. God created one woman for this one man, and the Bible says the two became one flesh. God chose how He wanted a marriage to be.

People sometimes make their own choices apart from what God wants, as I had regrettably done many times over outside of God's will. When we do, we are guaranteed to fail every single time. It says in God's Word, *"Except the Lord build the house, men do labor in vain to build it"* (Psalm 127:1a). Anything and everything I had built in the flesh, I had to maintain in the flesh. It wore me out, caused me grief and sadness, and through it all *the devil laughed at me* while keeping me emptyhanded and brokenhearted. Perhaps you can relate to what I am saying. For years, the devil stole from me, and most of the time it was done right under my nose.

My friend, please listen to what I am about to share that may help change your life. It's true, fools make a mock at sin, but in the end Satan or sin mocks the fool. Jesus said if we would *"seek and abide in His truth, His truth would make us free"* (see John 8:32).

I had labored many useless years in vain, the locusts had destroyed and devoured my life; but I am here to declare to you my friend, it's never too late to repent, seek mercy, find truth in Jesus, and allow the Holy Spirit to wash you clean with the blood of the Lamb. Allow Jesus Christ, the Son of the Living God, to cleanse you today from all your past sins, guilt and shame.

This I know: God is always good. God is a giver. He is merciful, slow to anger, and slow to wrath. He is always loving, always forgiving, and always ready to receive a contrite heart, one with sorrowful repentance. He will bring those contrite hearts into fullness of joy as they seek His truth, power and presence! Hallelujah! He also wants to give us the desires of our heart when our heart is set on fulltime obedience to His Word (see Psalm 37:4).

The true stories written in the Old Testament are written not just for a pleasurable read, but they are written for our own admonition. We can learn many valuable lessons concerning the children of Israel, and from the wisdom of the Holy Spirit as He flowed through the lives of many Old Testament prophets, priests and kings. There are so many helpful Scriptures filled with God's wisdom found all throughout the Bible. As you dig for treasures in God's Word, you'll find many words of wisdom in Ecclesiastes and Proverbs. Many of life's hard lessons can simply be avoided if we will hearken to the warnings, and learn to listen, trust, and obey the Word of God.

May we all have ears to hear and eyes to see; to believe God's Word, and apply it to our own life, so that we can be free to enjoy our lives by walking and living in liberty.

Remember this: There is always a reward for indulgence! Look past the gold ring, see the pig? That's the reward to those who lack discretion.

Proverbs 11:22 (KJV)

As a jewel of gold in a swine's snout, so is a fair woman which is without discretion.

Behold, I have set before you life and death. The choices you have made: Some were right, some were wrong. Under My Spirit of Grace, I have covered your mistakes. I love you. I came to help you, not to punish you. I came to rescue you from the hand of the enemy. Do you not know that My mercy triumphs over judgment? Have you not heard I neither sleep, nor slumber? Even though your heart may condemn you, I am greater than your heart. I am here with you now to strengthen you. Not one thing gets wasted from your past, not one thing. No matter how deep the trouble you have been in, no matter how much you struggled at times, I was working behind the scenes to bring you into a much deeper relationship with Me. I love you. I long for you to commune with Me. Take a walk with Me. Talk with Me about all that concerns you. For I can assure you, no harm shall be done unto you. You are My precious child. I am at work in your life. Take a look back; see how My arm is not too short that it cannot save. I tell you the Truth, you belong in My presence, and shall walk in My power.

Chapter Six

RISING ABOVE ADVERSITY

Around March of 2014, there was such an overwhelming desire put in me to go deeper in my walk with the Lord. I sensed He was calling me to limit my outside contact with the world, and go into what I will call my little cocoon. My life seemed to have no direction at all; I only existed, and at times even felt paralyzed and so alone. Although I was very busy doing things, and even doing many good things, I still felt so empty inside. There was such a huge void in my heart. Becoming really good at masking my pain in public was second nature for me.

Sometimes along our journey in life it may seem as if we're invisible, and no one really cares about how we are or what we may be going through. Although for many years I felt alone, the Lord was with me, watching over me. Many times when God speaks something to our hearts, like going off for months into a little cocoon, usually it makes no sense in the natural world.

At times I think it's okay to share what the Lord is speaking to me, but honestly and most likely, it will not be understood by the general public, and thus we must protect those precious thoughts and conversations we have privately with the Lord. We should hold those special conversations in our hearts, and only share with others as we are led by the Holy Spirit to share, not under pressure, and never to demean anyone.

Time invested with God is never lost time

Anytime we draw closer to the Lord, the enemy will be sure to oppose us, and try to get us off track. The devil will use anyone or everyone against us from making progress. If you have ever attempted to get quiet before the Lord, and search His truths out, just see how long it is before you get interrupted, either with some nagging thought, a phone call, bad news, disturbing interference, or noises. When that happens, just keep pressing into God, past the bad reports, the distractions, your pain, regrets, or failures, because He is your Answer! He is our great and exceeding reward (see Genesis 15:1 and Hebrews 11:6).

I want so much to share with you the truth about the amazing life we have when we seek the Lord first above anything else. There's no better source of strength than spending time in His Word and His presence. We truly can find fullness of joy while standing confidently in His presence, even when all hell seems to have broken loose over our lives. He offers pleasure triumphing over pain through a life hidden in Him, which includes abundant life now and forevermore (see Psalm 16:11 and John 10:10).

If you are a child of God, then you can go boldly to His throne of grace. Once there, you may obtain mercy, and find grace for any and every situation that you need help with. All you have to do is go in believing with faith in your heart, and you'll soon realize Jesus is your only true source of freedom. In Him you can live, you can be free to move, and find yourself all wrapped up in His faithfulness and loving kindness. You will find all that you need in His great love. He will never deny those who know in Whom they believe.

Many times over, while in my cocoon, I needed to make a conscious effort to not ignore my responsibilities or work, and not neglect natural things, but I desperately needed that set apart time, to get into the presence of Almighty God for help and answers. *This is why I was drawn into the Lord's hands: To allow Him to help give me strength and direction, while He was changing my heart in that cocoon.*

We all need to hear from God. I was absolutely desperate for change. I have shared only very small details about situations concerning my life. My life was hopeless prior to *The Triumphant Battle,* which I will share with you in a later chapter. Making the decision to spend as much time possible with the Lord, and not allow any outside interference to come in was a pretty easy decision for me. I didn't have many influences that could keep me from doing what I deemed in my heart as vital and necessary. God was leading me to do this. It's exactly what was needed. No human being was capable of giving me direction for my life. It's just better to go to the One who knows everything, and let Him work out His timing and plans for us.

Little did I know the path that I'd soon walk on was already there, done in the mind of God. He had a purpose, a greater plan, which permitted me to experience such grief and pain throughout my life. In the midst of it all, it's clearly seen now: He has given me a message of *faith, hope and love.* During many difficult years, I often prophesied over my life, and much of what I had been saying was about to come to pass. It included a great battle, which I never saw coming until the appointed time; clearly and concisely it was a battle marked: *Life or Death.*

It's important for you to know as you continue to read on, the gifts of the Holy Spirit are still in operation today, and are available for whosoever will believe on Jesus Christ as their personal Lord and Savior. We can learn to flow with Him as He manifests Himself to us by the power of the Holy Spirit. The Lord could even manifest through someone with the gifts of the Spirit, and that person may not even be aware of it! The Lord is unlimited in wisdom, glory and power, and He can do whatever He desires. When and how He manifests is all up to Him.

As I really sought after the Lord in my little cocoon, He began speaking to me through various ways. Sometimes, He would speak directly to me, and at other times it would be during a church service, through a godly inspired book or another person. The point isn't so much the method of

His communication, but we need to prepare our hearts to be ready to hear His voice, and reject all others.

One thing I heard during this precious time, the Lord said, "Pack up and weed out." I heard it several times throughout the day. I asked Him when I would be moving. Emphatically, He said, "Soon!" It was then that I knew, I was at the beginning of a brand new beginning, and was filled with such excitement and anticipation. I had very little money, very few resources, and absolutely no idea where I was going or what I would be doing, but I had a word from God!

Did you know that one word from God can change your entire life? Just one prophetic word or one word of encouragement can change your life forever! Believe me, I know! I am living proof that there really is a God who loves us, and who longs to be in a relationship with you and me.

During a long season of my life, I can remember so vividly that my prayers seemed to hit the ceiling and bounce right back. In addition to me feeling like my prayers weren't working, the whole world seemed to be arrayed against me. The devil can use anybody (sometimes even ones we love) to find a reason to judge or criticize our mistakes, when what is needed most is love, support and acceptance. Satan also can utilize demons to block or hinder our prayers. We must stay in communion with the Holy Spirit, and allow Him to reveal to us what may be trying to stop our progress. We can exercise our authority over the devil, and use that most wonderful name of Jesus to break those yokes of bondage and demonic forces trying to block our blessings and prayers.

Have you ever felt deeply depressed and wondered, if you died would anyone even care, and if they did, who would actually take time to attend your funeral? Have you ever had any crazy thoughts like that? If so, you're not alone. This is one of many common tactics that Satan uses to destroy people's lives, and gain entrance into their soul. Satan doesn't need your stuff, he wants your soul. If he can successfully ambush your soul, he can gain control over your will. If you lose the ability to exercise self-control, a fruit of the Spirit, he can successfully block your faith, which is needed to rise above adversity.

In order to successfully rise above adversity, I have had to learn *how* to guard my thoughts, and protect my love walk, which are entrance points into my soul. I haven't perfected it yet, but little by little, and from glory to glory, God is changing me into the likeness of His Son, Jesus Christ. Maintaining and developing a stronger love walk is one of the greatest challenges we the Church face today. *Guarding my soul by maintaining a healthy thought life, and protecting my love walk, have become some of the greatest weapons to recognizing the lies of the enemy!*

Knowing what you believe and why

My *"faith works by love,"* that's God's love in me working for, to and through me (see Galatians 5:6). One way to look at it is for me to recognize *"the love of God has already been shed abroad in my heart by the Holy Ghost"* (see Romans 5:5). It's His love flowing to me, working for me, and flowing in and through me that enables my faith to be operative faith, not dead faith. Faith is alive, and faith has a voice. Faith produces change, but I needed to learn also what to have faith in before seeing any lasting results. My faith is in the written Word of God. My faith is in the Holy Child, the Son of the Living God, Jesus Christ the Messiah. My faith is in His blood and in His Name. My faith is in the everlasting Almighty God and the Holy Spirit. My faith is believing every Word God has said is really true; no matter what circumstances may tell me otherwise.

I've been in various miracle meetings, and have heard a very well known and loved minister of the Gospel, Pastor Billy Burke say many times while he preaches, "We don't faith something to keep faithing it! No, we exercise our faith until we see it manifest! We walk by faith, not by sight that is true, but we faith it to see it come to pass in our lives. We want to feel, see, and experience what we are believing God for!" That is so true, dear friend. Hope is always future tense. Faith is now!

One way to keep our faith alive is to really believe you will see all that God has promised you come to pass! God is Faithful. Faith is always now, that means I must believe it now, ahead of time, before I see it with my natural eyes, or feel it with my physical senses. The world may say, "Show me, and I will believe," but we aren't of the world. We are in it, not of it.

The declaration of our faith is needed, especially when our physical senses have absolutely no evidence of what our hearts know is true. This reality of faith is required for breakthrough, and is a major component of how God has moved in my life with such miraculous power!

Have you realized there are many diverse voices in the world today, and none are without significance as recorded by the Apostle Paul, inspired by the Holy Spirit in First Corinthians 14:10? I sure have. It's not enough to know that the devil exists or that Jesus exists. It's not enough to have a little Bible trivia or knowledge. It's not enough to attend church once or twice a week, watch a Christian television program or listen to Christian music. It's not enough to guard what you watch on television or the type of movies you see. Unless we learn to cast down vain imaginations, and replace the lies that are coming into our minds with speaking the Word of God out of our mouths, we will continue to live defeated lives, and have a low life living mentality.

You may be familiar with the true account recorded in the Gospels, how after Jesus was baptized, the Holy Spirit descended upon Him. He was then led by the Holy Spirit into the wilderness to be tempted by the devil. The devil took Scriptures out of context, and quoted it to Jesus to try to tempt Him into sinning. What did Jesus do? He defeated the devil on every level, spirit, soul, and body by opening His mouth, and declaring truth of the written Word of God by saying, "It is written!" Jesus had to know what was written, what it meant, how it was rightly divided, and then He had to say something out of His mouth. He didn't just think the problem or the lies of the devil away.

There are many instances in the Bible that bear out that our faith must speak. Your faith has a voice, and my faith has a voice. I have learned that the more I open my mouth, and declare or prophecy the Word of the Lord over my life; He will come on the scene, and deliver me out of the snare of the enemy. I must keep my faith alive and active, while exercising my authority as a believer over the devil, and guarding my love walk. There are many Scriptures to validate these principles.

These two Scriptures emphasize how important it is to *believe and act upon* the Word by speaking our faith out loud:

"I believed, therefore have I spoken" (Psalm 116:10a KJV).

"We having the same spirit of faith, according as it is written, I believed; and therefore have I spoken; we also believe and therefore speak" (Second Corinthians 4:13 KJV).

Gaining spiritual strength

As a direct result of taking that much needed time in my little cocoon, I have become stronger spiritually now than ever before. That doesn't mean that I can take time off, the devil is always looking for a moment of weakness, or for me to let my guard down. That doesn't mean that I am immune to the enemy's attacks, but I have gained a new level of spiritual strength that I didn't have before.

Another thing that was revealed during that time, is how to better recognize (discern) the enemy's lies, and detect his subtle, enticing voice. Now when attacks come, I am better prepared. There is such a huge benefit of being prepared ahead of time. Praying in other tongues in my own heavenly prayer language (also known as praying in the Spirit) with heartfelt prayers is one of the ways that helps safeguard my position, and not lose ground that I have taken back that the devil had stolen from me. I've learned that I really can overcome the devil's schemes, and always be steps ahead of him. It takes work and dedication. It takes praying in my known language, and also in my heavenly prayer language. It takes sacrifice to study the Word of God.

In addition to those things, declaring the Word of God out loud over my life has also benefitted me tremendously. Like King David, we are to be stirring ourselves up, encouraging ourselves in the Lord. It's helped me so much to continue speaking His truth over my life, especially when circumstances dictated otherwise. Even if an assault comes now unexpectedly, I can still say with full confidence that I know, *that I really know*, God is at work; it is well with my soul, and confess out loud, that I believe *ALL* things are working together for my good, and for God's glory. It doesn't have to look good, feel good, or seem good to the natural mind, but if I keep up my faith in what the Word of God promises me, I know in the end I will win every single time.

We can frame our world by speaking forth His Word, and when God is ready to move, surely you will know when He has been there! When we begin to declare what God has said about us, not man, and recognize the enemy's deceptive tactics, we can begin walking in a brand new level of freedom.

If you want to gain more victory in your life, and conquer the devil at every temptation or trial, keep your heart and mouth hooked up with the Lord. He will always see you through to the other side. You, too, can say like the Apostle Paul, *"I know Whom I have believed"* (see Second Timothy 1:12).

I will meet all your needs.

I will become your dreams.

I will fulfill your desires.

Look to Me for your inspiration, look to Me for all things.

Allow Me to take you higher into the place I've created for you. Your wounds have been opened so that I could pour My healing balm into your soul. Take a look around at those ashes that have fallen off of you. For you stand before Me untainted, in My holiness, in My beauty, and you see My splendor and grace manifesting with eyes unveiled.

Joyfully submit, surrender with joy. Arise, shine, move ahead; go ahead and take that step I have ordered for you. It's safe, and I've declared it to be "Good!"

Listen, trust, and obey My voice, and no other.

Chapter Seven

THE PROPHETIC VOICE

It was June 2006, and was time for me to start over once again with no idea where to begin. As shared earlier, I was raised and grew up with a Baptist background, and am thankful for the basic doctrine I learned about the Gospel, and the Bible scriptures that I was taught to memorize as a child. In addition, I'm very thankful for those teachers in my church that showed me love, but I personally never felt like I was making any progress in my own life. Many churches I attended or visited seemed to be filled with people who were lukewarm, critical and judgmental. I needed to find God's love and understanding for myself to get back on my feet again.

In desperation one morning I cried out to God, and earnestly sought His direction to lead me to a new church where I could be fed properly, and grow with a body of believers who were really on fire and passionate about the things of God. Having been introduced to the gifts of the Holy Spirit, many questions arose in my mind as I had never heard, nor been taught about these things before; questions that I wasn't able to get answers to from the traditional places of worship I once attended.

The Lord spoke to me that morning. It was one of the first times ever I can vividly remember hearing His voice. Many times prior, I often wondered if God heard my prayers. For so long it seemed as if my prayers were hollow, and went unanswered. I don't blame God. Since then, I have learned that we need to pray according to His Word, which is His will, and He does hear, and will grant us the petitions we desire of Him (see First John 5:14).

The Lord said to me that He wanted me to go to a particular church where I had once seen a famous lady preacher as a guest speaker, and start attending that church. I was excited and shocked all in the same moment. I couldn't believe God spoke back to me! My next question to the Lord was asking Him how I would ever find this church, because it had been a long time since I had been there, and I didn't know the name of it or where it was located.

Later that same morning, I was out at a local pharmacy. A woman who appeared like she had been crying came up to me, and complimented me on my makeup. I thought that was strange seeing how I hardly had on any makeup that day, but I thought to myself, God must have sent her to me for a reason. As we began talking, she told me that she and her husband were having difficulties, and she was hoping to get some new makeup to try to look pretty for him. I asked her where she had just come from, because it was so evident that her tears were fresh. She said she had just come from a house of prayer. I inquired and asked, "A house of prayer? What's that?" She said, "It's something my church does on Saturday mornings. We go there and seek the Lord in prayer."

I was so concerned for this lady, and wanted to show her God's love, and honestly wasn't even thinking about my prayer request that was made earlier that morning. I asked her what the name of her church was. She told me, and as she did, it was as if those words she spoke came to life, and went right through me. I had a strong knowing on the inside that this was the church God was leading me to. Just to confirm, I asked the lady if she knew if this famous lady minister had ever preached at her church before. She of course said, "Yes!" and then gave me directions.

I had just gone through many trials myself, and had recently relocated several hours away from where I used to live. Being in a new area, I didn't know many people, and wasn't at all familiar with my surroundings. The Lord gave me a supernatural, divine connection that morning to help point me toward the path He had already prepared for me to walk on ahead of time.

God knows the secret desires of all our hearts. He knows our thoughts, He guides our footsteps, and He leads us into His plan when we seek after His will. We simply need to seek Him with our whole heart, listen for His voice, and then take that step of faith. He will show up and show off in some of the most unbelievable ways just because He can! Our God is a wondrous-working God!

After visiting that church I didn't have to look any further. It was exactly what I needed for the season I was in. It was exciting to learn about the gifts of the Spirit, the prophetic voice, and many other spiritual gifts, too. Sitting under their teaching helped me learn about prophecy, and how hearing just one word from God could change my life. What I had before wasn't getting me any closer to God. Breakthrough was needed for a fresh start.

They would sometimes have guest speakers come in and minister to us. Many times, this one guest speaker in particular would come periodically over the years. He was anointed by God as a New Testament prophet. He spoke as the Spirit would lead him with words of encouragement, exhortation and comfort. Through his ministry I saw people also get deliverance from demons. Many times as he would come and visit, he would prophecy over me, and give a confirming word, something that the Lord was already dealing with me about; but then at other times, I would get a new word! Wow! That was exciting! Some of those words have already come to pass. Some are in the works now. Others I have put on a shelf for the appointed time.

As I began to develop an ear to hear and eyes to see, I was able to better discern the Lord's voice. Obviously, I missed it many times past, as revealed by former choices and experiences I have shared. In doing so, by developing our spiritual ears and eyes, we can also learn to recognize the voice of the enemy as we spend more time with the Lord. It's not as easy today for the devil to get one over on me; not saying that he can't, because that would be foolish to think that I couldn't be deceived. *We all can be hoodwinked or fooled.* It's so important for us to spend time communing with our heavenly Father, to enjoy the presence of our Lord Jesus Christ, and have fellowship with the person, the Holy Ghost. I used to be a banker. Spotting counterfeits was one of my specialties. How could I recognize them so fast? I spent years and years with the genuine.

An authentic promise

In November of 2013, the Lord gave me a new prophetic Word: *"Restitution."* It's one of the most outstanding words I have ever received from the Lord. I wasn't even sure what the word *"Restitution"* meant and had to look it up. According to *Merriam-Webster's* dictionary the definition of the word is:

Definition of ¹restitution

1: an act of restoring or a condition of being restored: as

a: a restoration of something to its rightful owner

b: a making good of or giving an equivalent for some injury

2: a legal action serving to cause restoration of a previous state

When I received this promise from the Lord, at that particular point in time, everything in my life had been stolen from me. The devil had stolen my dignity, worth, value, money, health, property, love and many other things. There are so many cases in point, but for the sake of time, I will mention just a couple.

My home was lost in a wrongful foreclosure. A well-known bank prequalified me over the phone to lower my interest rate to help me save my home, and sent me a loan modification agreement with supporting documents. I had fallen behind on the monthly payments, and was doing everything possible to keep afloat. The bank agreed to process my loan application, as long as I could verify I had enough income to support the newly-proposed, lower monthly mortgage payment.

With much negotiation, they made an exception with a stipulation. If I was able to lease my home, to help supplement the income needed, and overnight them a copy of said lease, along with a check for the new proposed payment amount, they would be able to grant my loan modification, and I could proceed into the initial trial period. What they asked for seemed absolutely impossible! I was attending school full time out of state, the house was vacant, plus I had no idea how to advertise, show, and lease my home within their deadline of less than one week.

A very long story short, a prayer partner prayed with me over the telephone believing God for a miracle. The prayer line I contacted was available through a well-known ministry, who teaches *Faith*, believes the Bible, and is used by God in many miraculous ways. Within the allotted timeframe, I was able to produce all the criteria they demanded as necessary to move forward with the loan modification. As a condition, there was a short trial period in which I had to continue making the newly reduced monthly payments on time with a certified bank check, and was successful in doing so with this newly generated income from the lease. After successfully completing the trial process, I would be granted final approval, and the loan modification would be completed. I was so thankful that what seemed to be such an impossible, daunting task was now behind me. I could keep my home and make the payments, since the tenants were paying on time.

Life seemed good until one day I noticed that my cashier's check hadn't cleared the bank for my mortgage payment. I was concerned, because I always paid ahead of time, and wanted to ensure no late payments. Many months had passed where I had paid as agreed, and I was through the initial trial period, so I contacted the bank to find out if they had received my payment, or if I needed to resend. To my surprise, they received it on time, however; they were not going to apply it to my loan.

The customer service representative said he had to ask me a question as my loan account had been flagged. What was said just about blew me away. He asked if I was living in my home or not. I kind of laughed, because I thought he was really kidding. I explained to him that he needed to review his file, and the obvious should have been clear, since it was approved subject to proof of a new lease to increase my income. I asked him several times to apply my payment. I explained to him that my mailing address where all of the loan modification documents had been sent to me was out of state, where I was residing at the time. In addition, the loan application had my out of state address on it. It's was the underwriter's final hoop to jump through, for me to produce a lease; that was their condition for final approval that I had to meet.

As it was explained to him, as impossible as all that was to obtain, I did exactly what they required; and I was able to get my income to debt ratio within their said guidelines, plus paid as agreed. After a long, drawn out battle with the bank, they eventually foreclosed on my property. Because I wasn't living in the home, they claimed they could deny my loan modification, even though they knew I wasn't living in it from the beginning; even though I had successfully passed the initial trial period. Eventually, I couldn't fight it anymore, and lost my home.

Please know I had every intention to pay my obligations. I did absolutely everything within my power to maintain my credit, and pay what I owed. It saddens me that in one of my greatest times of need, I was led astray to believe that they were really trying to help me save my home. Later on I discovered that I was only one of many people, who this big bank wrongfully foreclosed on. I received a small compensation from the Office of the Comptroller of the Currency, who after reviewing my case sent a letter with a check, which inferred that I had been wrongfully treated. Even after the O.C.C. concluded researching my file, the said bank that did this, stands on their vague opinions of having done no wrong; although they won't respond to my petitions for answers with straight replies.

Since that time, I have let it go in my heart, and believe that God's justice is enough. The world system is full of people who yield to the enemy of our souls, and will lie, steal, and cheat, because that's the devil's plan for all mankind. Many are used as weapons against us for the destruction of our lives, but I have been promised *"Restitution"* ...*and know, it's mine!*

Going back a little further, I had been in a car accident in 2006. The lady who struck my vehicle didn't even know she was on a one-way street as she was from out of state. When it came down to it, the insurance companies didn't want to pay for all the damages assessed with that accident. A very long story short, I didn't get a nickel. There was a gruesome, five day battle in court, and even though I had to have lower back surgery, suffered with extensive whiplash, and missed a lot of work, they still didn't budge. My quality of life was completely altered and interrupted. I had to have months of therapy, but somehow they managed to find a way to convince the jury that I didn't deserve anything, and that's what I got - nothing.

Shortly after that defeat in the courtroom, I received a notification that the insurance companies were suing me for approximately $78,000.00 for court and legal related costs. I couldn't believe it! I borrowed $10,000.00 to appeal, however; my appeal never even got answered properly. Their convoluted answer didn't even make sense, and it wasn't even clear that my appeal had been denied. My appellate attorney wanted another large sum of money to pursue it further. Years later, I still had no ability to repay those court related costs. In the end, they settled with me when I offered them several thousand dollars as full payment.

The Lord fights our battles, and sometimes bad things happen to good people. We don't have all the answers this side of Heaven. One of the most blessed things that transpired through that entire painful process is this: One man's life was changed. One of the attorney's at the firm that was helping me was won to Jesus Christ. I led him in a prayer of salvation over the telephone several years after the verdict had come in, and he confessed Jesus as His Lord and Savior. I borrowed the money, paid the amount agreed upon to settle, and thank God it's over.

That prophetic word "*Restitution*" is mine! I don't have to see it with my natural eyes to believe it in my heart. God always comes through for me. He always makes His Word manifest in my life. It may not be in my timing, but in His time *everything* is made beautiful. His Word never fails, and always prevails over my life.

Heaven's answers manifest

During time spent in my cocoon, the Lord said many things to me concerning my life. He showed me areas of weakness that I needed to strengthen, and taught me so many incredible lessons. One of the things the Lord was teaching me about was not going back to the arm of Pharaoh. Do you know what I mean by that? Not to return back to Egypt, or said another way, the bondage of man.

Up until that point in my life I had a very jaded outlook toward most men. Most of which I came into contact with only validated my thoughts, and reinforced their selfishness or inability to tell the truth. Some would try to pull me away from the things of God. Most of them subtracted from my life; it wasn't added to. The Lord was warning me to not return to that specific bondage.

The Lord spoke to me one day while I was taking out the trash. While I was walking down the sidewalk He said, "If he doesn't see you as a valuable treasure, he (no matter who he is) is not worth your time." Those words pierced my heart. I knew exactly what that meant. By this time, I had now been through many failed relationships, and was at the point of no return. I knew that I could never trust anyone ever again. Continuously, I had settled for less than God's best throughout my entire adult life, and every time got exactly what I had settled for. Right, wrong or indifferent, I kept getting enticed by the devil with wrong thinking about myself and others. Satan was a master of performing the most perfect "set ups" to lure me again and again into his traps of disillusionment.

Satan is a liar and a thief. His only mission is to cause mankind to fail, and be trodden under foot. Remember that verse from Proverbs from an earlier chapter? I failed over and over to look past the gold ring (Satan's master disillusionment) in order to see the swine it was attached to, and that for my indulgence (into sin) was my reward. I have no one to blame for my bad choices, except the devil through his deception, and in some cases my flesh.

I am not neglecting my personal responsibilities or disqualifying my ability to choose right from wrong, but am simply pointing out that in many cases, I was deceived about who and what people really were upfront. Sometimes true colors didn't surface until I was in over my head. Yes, it stands to reason I should have done more due diligence upfront, and should have taken more needed time when making life altering decisions. It never helps when we are rushed, conned, or pressured into making choices that may have severe consequences.

Regardless of past mistakes, I am not defined or bound to them any longer. On a regular basis, it helps me to declare that I am not ignorant of the devil's devices. It hinders him from occupying any place in my life, because I don't want to be kidnapped again into his webs of deception. *The traps he sets for us are always extremely enticing to our flesh, soul and senses.*

Wise as serpents, gentle as doves

Some of you may know this, but for the sake of others who don't… It's good to understand when pressure comes, the heat is on, and you haven't heard from God on the matter; that's *not* the right time to make major decisions that can cause permanent damage.

Jesus Christ loves His Bride, the Church. Jesus would never rush or pressure us, tell a lie, cheat, mislead, or physically abuse that which He loves.

Men are commanded by God to love their wives, and wives are commanded to respect their husbands. When the leader of the home fails to carry out this commandment, everything he's connected to becomes affected. If we are unevenly yoked in relationships *(especially while dating)* things can develop into dangerous soul ties before we even realize it. You can be sure then those types of things we despise most will eventually manifest and show up. Those are the counterfeits, and they are in extreme contrast and exact opposite of God's best.

We can only receive total healing and restoration from life's hard lessons or experiences through God's love and His power to forgive us for all past wrongdoings. That's what brings us total healing, restoration, freedom and deliverance. Time alone cannot heal all wounds, but receiving God's grace, His mercy, love, and forgiveness *can* in time bring forth complete healing. God didn't lead me into any harmful relationships. I had not only sinned against my own body, but I had sinned against the Lord. He doesn't lead us into sin, because He said in His Word that He is not the one who tempts us.

It's so important to understand He will never bless that which He didn't authorize. *"Except the Lord build the house we labor in vain to build it" (Psalm 127:1a).* He is the author and finisher of our faith, and anything that is not of faith is sin (see Hebrews 12:2 and Romans 14:23). We shouldn't expect the Lord to bless anything we create apart from Him. It should be said again. The Lord never has to bless that which He didn't authorize or commence. His blessings were not upon any of my past failed relationships.

The black cloud syndrome seemed to follow me everywhere. I was living under a severe curse. I didn't understand it all those years, but that's exactly what was going on. I had given the enemy permission to come in and trespass due to ignorance, but in some cases he came in through willful sin. Then he did what he's always done. He came in to steal, kill and destroy; stealing my dignity, worth and value. Satan kept me in the dark about who I really was as a child of God in Christ Jesus. In addition, he killed my joy; I was one of the most depressed people I knew. I didn't even like myself most of the time. Satan destroyed my self-esteem, confidence and self-worth.

Due to my history, it has made it extremely difficult for me to believe anyone. Satan is my arch enemy, and apparently knew God had a good plan for my life before I did. The devil did *everything* in his power to keep me from receiving it. During my entire life he worked tirelessly to block my blessings, and keep me in bondage, full of regret and absent of life.

You may or may not agree, but I believe that God dislikes divorce *if* the two people *He has joined together* decide to go their own way and separate. However; I also believe His heart is grieved when His children disobey His rules, and just run off, and do their own thing outside of His will. My life could be likened to that of the prodigal son. I was doing my own thing, enticed through the lust of my own flesh, and giving place to the wrong voices either through ignorance or wrongful consent.

Do you think God would hate divorce if two gays or lesbians got married, then divorced? Would God hate it then? What if one of those people were once a Christian, who backslid and got deceived about who they were in Christ, and then made the decision to join civilly in marriage with a partner of the same sex? Would God hate for them to correct a wrong to make it right through divorce? Absolutely not!

God loves people. He loves all people, every color, every tribe, every tongue and every nation. He loves men and women, boys and girls. He isn't interested in human labels, but He is interested in the eternity that He's placed in man's heart. God is a lover of people, but He doesn't condone sin. I read in Proverbs, *"These six things doth the LORD hate: yea, seven are an abomination unto Him"* (Proverbs 6:16). Divorce didn't make the cut. Some religious folks will say with their pointed finger of criticism, "God *hates* divorce." Some of these religious spirits love to criticize when they have absolutely no knowledge of intimate details in a person's marriage, which may include physical or sexual abuse, infidelity, or many other vile things that may surround a situation that demands a reasonable cause for divorce.

Someone once told me while I was trapped in an abusive relationship with a con artist, "You've made your bed, now sleep in it." They offered no help to me, none at all. They believed that the situation I was in, no matter how bad it was, I had no choice but to remain a silent victim, and endure the suffering of my poor choice. Even though they didn't have all the violent details, they had enough information that they could have just offered to pray for me. Aren't you glad God looks at the heart, and knows every detail of our painful situations we sometimes find ourselves in? I know I sure am.

Sometimes we fail to recognize our own sin, perhaps for some of us it's lusting over a beautiful woman or attractive man, which if taken too far can develop into the sin of fornication or adultery. Others may like to gossip and slander those who seek after holiness and purity. Some people are so quick to give their opinion about God, but are void of knowing His Word. God is good. We all fall short of His glory, but thank God when we become truly born again we are sealed with the Holy Spirit, and are being transformed into the image of His Son, Jesus Christ.

Working out my own salvation is a continual process in my life today. I have to renew my mind daily, and fully be aware I am only one step away from a wrong choice. Acknowledging I'm far from perfect, relying on His unfailing love and mercy, and being close to Jesus has helped me get through difficult times of testing, temptations and trials. Thank God, provision has been made for us when we as believers do make mistakes and sin (see First John 1:9). He's after our pure heart, not our works or deeds to gain His love and acceptance through a perfect performance.

Equally, it's important to know grace is not an excuse to live habitually in sin, but grace is *always, always, always* given for our deliverance from bondage, not to keep us in it! God is a God of love, mercy, hope, healing and forgiveness. Some religious people may disagree, and be there to point their fingers making snide remarks and passing judgment, but it's only the blood of Jesus that makes one free from the slanders of man. Perhaps they should consider reading Matthew 7:7, where it says, *"We are to judge not, lest we, too, shall be judged."* The Bible says to fear the Lord, to fear the One who can send your soul to hell, not man. I am going with what the Bible says about God. He is a lover of people, a God of justice, and also our Great Deliverance. Nothing and no one can ever separate us from the love of God, not our past pain, past failures or former shame.

His mercy endures forever

Not long ago, I was living in bondage, and was in a wilderness of shame, just like the Israelites had once been. They got delivered from Egypt, but lived in bondage for forty years making the same mistakes over and over. God's grace was available back then. He had a way for them to repent, and get their life right to walk in holiness and purity before the Lord their God. However; their bad choices many times led them down the wrong path.

One thing that needs said, in God's eyes, obedience is better than sacrifice according to His Word (see First Samuel 15:22). Whatever we do in the flesh, if our hearts are in disobedience to God's will, then whatever we do apart from God's will *ALWAYS* has to be maintained in the flesh. *Sadly heartache, disappointment, and consequences come as a result of choices made in the flesh, rather than in the Spirit.*

Just like King Saul was not part of God's original plan for the Israelites, His people suffered many consequences due to their sinful desires, leading them away from God's plan; yet they wanted to live in the flesh, and be like the world. Remember Adam and Eve's sin in the Garden of Eden? Their disobedience brought severe consequences to man.

Did you know the Bible says that God created Eve and took her to Adam? He made Adam just one wife. It may stand to reason that God has a special unity for two specific people, unless of course, they are called to remain single. God didn't create three women and one man. He didn't create two men, either. He created Adam first, then Eve.

It would make our lives so much easier if we were willing to listen to God's Word and obey the Lord. Oh, if I just could have waited for His good plan to unfold in my life, then so many sleepless nights and countless tears could have been avoided. Thank God for His mercy! I don't know about you, but I had to learn a few hard lessons before my heart changed into one to be quick to obey. The consequences for disobedience are severe, and people's lives can be shipwrecked and damaged along the way.

My desire now is to help others better recognize their enemy, the devil. Perhaps you or someone you know can identify with what I have gone through. We can overcome wrong thinking patterns by understanding where a lot of our thoughts and ideas come from, and begin renewing our minds daily to the Word of God. We can conquer the devil, take back what's been stolen from us, and start walking in victory today!

The past is past, it's time to heal

In September of 2014, I mentioned earlier that I heard from the Lord that I was to begin the process of packing up and weeding out. He also said, "Out with the old, in with the new," and as a declaration of my faith, I agreed and thanked the Lord out loud for the new beginnings that were ahead of me. I was heading out of state to a women's conference at the end of the month, and knew upon my return I would begin taking those steps. Right before I left for my trip, I shared with someone that the Lord spoke to me, and that I was unsure about when and where I was going. I had no other details other than the simple instructions to pack up and weed out.

As we were talking they prophetically said to me, "The Israelites had to circumcise their men prior to entering into their promised land. All the things that you have experienced brought you to this place in time, they were indeed painful and bloody, just like it was for the Israelite men. You needed time to heal, but it (that difficult and painful process) was necessary, and now you are getting ready to walk into your promised land." They encouraged me with those words from the Lord. We prayed together, and asked God to lead and direct my path so I could enter into my promised land. I had no idea how good this "promised land" would be. Like Joshua and Caleb, I too, had to defeat many giants in order to go in and possess my land.

Interestingly enough, I had lunch about a year earlier with this same person that prayed with me about entering into my promised land. During our lunch she said by the Holy Ghost that God was speaking to me, and the next time I got married, God was going to hold me accountable for my actions to my husband. She said all the past mistakes and failed marriages were in essence covered under the blood of Jesus. In other words, I was washed clean from all my past sins through my faith in the blood of Jesus and repentance. I got so upset. Who would even dare say such a ridiculous thing that I would ever get married again? I was absolutely floored. Quickly, I dismissed those words as a "false" prophecy, and thought to myself: *I was never getting married again, so that certainly wouldn't ever be an issue!*

God's greater glory about to be revealed

On January 9, 2015, I attended a special healing and miracle meeting in North Miami Beach, Florida. Again, I received another special prophetic word from the Lord spoken through Pastor Billy Burke. The Lord said through him, "Hungry you are. Hungry you are, hungry for more. He's about to prosper you beyond your wildest dream." Little did I know that those words would quickly come to pass in my life. When that Word came every circumstance surrounding my life in the natural dictated otherwise.

There are many voices in the world, none without significance. You must become one with Me, spend quality time in My presence so that you will learn to know My voice.

Voices calling you here, voices calling you there; you must keep your eyes fixed strait upon Me. You must learn to abide in Me. You must learn to cling to Me.

You must guard our time together. Come closer to hear My voice. Come up higher so that you can embrace My love for you.

In this place of shelter, under Me, you're abiding under My shadow. I am the Lord your God, the Almighty God, the Everlasting God, and I will protect you from the wicked one. Just abide, abide, abide in Me. Let My words abide in you, and you shall know the Truth of every matter.

My logos Word shall then become Rhema to you. My words will be more real to you than your circumstances. When you prophecy to your circumstances according to My word, you shall see change at the right time, right before your eyes. Stay steady, move ahead. Do not quit, do not give up; for I am with you, going before you, fighting for you, and I am the Lord your God.

Chapter Eight

THE TRIUMPHANT BATTLE

It was late December of 2014, I was right smack dab in the middle of packing up and weeding out when someone contacted me, and asked if I had been on Facebook lately. They wondered if I knew that one of my high school friends had been in the hospital. I had no idea since I wasn't a big user of Facebook; time spent there was limited. I messaged my friend who was in the hospital to let them know that I was praying for them and wished them well. Then a reply came back asking if I had kept up on any news concerning my high school sweetheart, Mike. My answer was, "No." It was that day I learned that Mike had recently lost his wife in November of 2014. My friend suggested that I reach out to him to let him know I would be praying for him.

Without much thought, I simply sent a friend's request to him. Some time had passed. A message from him came back in response to my friend's request. In essence it said he didn't want to seem rude, but he couldn't accept my friend's request. Mike briefly explained how he was going through a difficult time. I could tell by his response he really didn't want anything to do with me. His response was okay with me; I figured I would just pray for him. He didn't really need to know how often or how sincere I was.

Remembering that day, I was deeply moved in my spirit with such grief to think that he was going through this tragedy all alone. I knew him very well at one time. We were both loners, so I just assumed he was trying to manage the best he could by himself.

On Christmas Day, 2014, as I sat across the table with one of my girlfriends, periodically I kept checking my phone for any new messages from Mike. As I shared my story with her, I explained who Mike was to me; how we dated over a period of six years, and had been engaged three times, but never made it to the alter. I told her out of all the people I had dated, he was the only one that held that special place in my heart.

Briefly while we talked, I shared how he kept cheating on me with the same girl, and because of how angry it made me, it's what led me to move to Florida to get a fresh start. Even though these painful memories came up that day, I sensed in my spirit that Mike was really in trouble, and I began carrying a much heavier weight; I can't really explain it in mere human words. It was heavy and oppressive. It was supernatural.

The story of our breakup was a familiar story to me. No matter where I went or who I would talk to for the past twenty plus years, Mike's name always came up as the one guy that I really loved that rejected me for somebody else. All those years later, the feelings of sadness, abandonment and rejection never left; unfortunately, I could never let him go from my heart either. Even though I was the one who moved out of state when I was twenty-one, I always wished that things would have been different.

What's ironic is that *only two months prior* to this time on October 18, 2014, which happened to be Mike's birthday, I had gotten moving boxes and brought them home so I could start weeding out and packing up. I marked this significant achievement down on one of my poster boards to keep myself motivated to take another step and move ahead. Around that same time, I had been going through old photos, and came across a picture of Mike and me. It was our first Easter together taken in 1987. I had several pictures of us from Easter that I had been holding on to.

Even though it was painful to look at our pictures, I could never seem to part with those memories. I only looked at them occasionally, but every single time I did it was with such deep regret. We were so happy together in those pictures. Over the years I often wondered what had happened to Mike. I often wondered if he still thought about me. I often wondered if he still loved me. What we had was real. What we had was a rare and special treasure. We fell in love as young kids, but we were so deeply in love with one another. We were inseparable, two peas in a pod; knowing if we had gotten into a fight we'd always get back together, or so we both thought.

As a step of faith in obedience to the Lord around the middle of October 2014, I looked at our pictures one last time before tearing them up and throwing them away. The Lord had also said, "Out with the old, in with the new," and I felt a gentle nudge that I should go ahead, and move on with my life. Then I reasoned that I should stop feeling so brokenhearted over someone I would *never see again.* In the trash torn up they went. With heaviness in my heart, I decided to move on and kept weeding out.

Having broken out of my cocoon, I decided I was going to fully surrender my life, and was committed one hundred percent to do whatever it was that God wanted me to do. For the record, it was decided I would do it alone. That's what was going through my mind while I was packing up to move. There was no need to get involved with anyone else. Why put myself through more disappointment and heartache? I was so tired of failed relationships; I just figured God wanted me to be alone. I was really okay with that. I didn't necessarily like to be alone all the time, but I wanted to pursue the call and dreams in my heart more than anything else.

Once in a while I would have dreamy thoughts and wish that "Mr. Right" was out there somewhere, and somehow he would come to my rescue. Then I would come back to my senses and weigh it out: Be alone and be happy, or be in another relationship and be miserable. With much pondering, I figured anyone that I would meet would not be able to get on board, and allow me to do what I wanted to do for the Lord anyway, so it made sense to be alone. Most people like comfort, and are so set in their ways, the chances of any "Mr. Right" being out there for me was slim to none. Being alone and empty inside seemed to be my lot in life, and I learned to accept it. More than anything, even above my own feelings, all I really wanted to do was God's will, and He knew that.

Journaling is one thing I really enjoy doing, especially keeping track of words that the Lord gives me. I have learned over the years like the prophet Samuel, to not let one Word of God fall to the ground. It's so important to keep His words in front of us and speak them out loud; whatever it is that God speaks to our hearts.

On December 1, 2014, a prophetic utterance came forth and I said, *"The Word of God springs forth life out of my mouth."* It was bold and emphatic. I wrote it down on my poster board, and whenever I would look at it I would declare it out loud. It brings great encouragement to rehearse what God has said, because the devil is always right there trying to get us to change our confessions.

There are many reasons He kept me hidden in that cocoon for a season. In part it was for an upcoming special assignment; one that I had no idea was coming. Little did I know that truly the Word of God would be springing forth life out of my mouth. He had been preparing me ahead of time, for what He knew I would need in order to do spiritual warfare in the very near future.

A few days passed since I heard from Mike. I had been praying often throughout the days for him. Then a message came, and he was reconsidering having conversation with me through Facebook. He was very distant, his thoughts were scattered, and it was conveyed he couldn't trust anyone else or himself. He was very broken to say the least. He was extremely vulnerable, and I knew I had to be very cautious as to what I said. His guard was up; at least it was up to the best of his ability. Knowing how vulnerable he would be wasn't anything I could have ever anticipated or just got ready for overnight. To say that he was fragile and weak would be an understatement. He seemed suicidal, and probably had it not of been that he had a little girl to take care of, he might have given up. In my heart of hearts, I knew the Lord had prepared me to help him fight a battle. It was a battle for his life. The enemy of his soul was on a mission: *Death and Destruction.*

Our first conversations

We had been messaging back and forth for several days, and something surfaced that I was not at all expecting. Mike shared with me how over the years at different times he had prayed for me, wished that I was well, and had hoped that I was happy in life. He would go in and out of somewhat normal type conversations while he was dealing with grief and loss. Satan had been working overtime on his mind, and at times he spoke as a child would. He seemed completely unstable most of the time, and said things that are expected when people experience a significant loss. His soul was being tormented day and night. After the initial shock of his words that he had hoped I had been happy in life wore off, it made me angry. I thought, how in the world could he *possibly* have said something so contradictory to our past breakup? I mean, come on! He was the one who had the problem cheating on me, or so I thought. I was floored. We dialogued back and forth pertaining to this topic for a while. There was much frustration on both ends.

Conquering my soul to silence concerning relationships had been my new normal for quite some time. With lots of material and experiences to go by, it was manageable being alone. While sharing with Mike the many valid reasons behind the "why" of me not ever wanting to trust men again, it definitely came as a big surprise to him.

Some of the horrific things we discussed he never thought could happen to me. He said it made him very sad that I hadn't found happiness. The more he tried to sympathize with me the angrier I became. Without warning, he then went on a rampage about how relationships are supposed to work, and that made me even angrier. It seemed like nonsense and gibberish to me at the time. What was spoken sounded ridiculous, and I had no living proof that trusting anyone was ever of any benefit. Dreams and fantasies like that didn't even exist in my mind anymore.

Previously from time to time, I admitted I had those dreamy thoughts or ideas about meeting the right person, but I can honestly say those thoughts were completely destroyed and nonexistent by this time. The decision had already been made, and I wasn't ever going to let anyone into my life again.

Time plus pain had made me extremely hardhearted toward relationships. I didn't want anything to do with a boyfriend (or husband) on any level, not even friendship. I wasn't in a place to be able to hear anyone tell me anything about relationships. The protective walls I had built around me were strong, tall and impenetrable.

True love never dies

Although my love for Mike never ceased over the years he had no knowledge of it, and I wasn't about to let the cat out of the bag. He didn't need to know that then; besides it wouldn't have been right for me to bring any personal feelings into our initial conversations, and I didn't. He didn't need to know I had just recently thrown away our pictures that I had kept all those years. What he needed most was help and understanding. He didn't need someone from his past trying to play with his emotions, and string his heart along.

What he knew was what I displayed toward him; empathy coupled with unconditional patience. I treated him the same way I would a stranger that I was ministering to, and surrounded him constantly with faith and God's love. We mutually agreed upfront after our initial conversation over the telephone, that we most definitely needed boundaries in our conversations if we were going to continue any type of discussions going forward. Boundaries in our conversations were of the utmost necessity.

It was my heart's desire to share the love of God with him, and reflect the unconditional love of Jesus Christ. That was my daily goal. Deep within my spirit I knew he was extremely fragile, and I needed to keep my personal feelings out of the equation. I was on a special assignment by the Holy Spirit to help pull him out of the living hell he was experiencing.

Truth revealed

Within approximately twenty-four hours of our initial telephone conversation, in which I accused Mike of cheating on me with the same girl repeatedly, we spoke again on the telephone. I will never forget the supernatural event that took place that day. I had been laboring in much prayer day and night for Mike as he was so weak and unstable. My heart grieved for him, and constantly I was feeling helpless; I really had to lean on God for strength and hope while I was praying. His battle was undeniably a matter of life and death. It seemed cruel and horrific what he was going through.

His mind was constantly under attack, but what he was about to reveal to me changed my life in a split second. He said he had been thinking about our conversation, and was troubled by the fact that I had left him, moved away and never saw him again, because I claimed he kept cheating on me. He said that he *never* cheated on me. That was the whole basis of why I relocated out of state! I was totally convinced beyond a shadow of a doubt he had rejected me, wanted someone else, and couldn't ever be trusted again.

The awakening of my soul

Keep in mind that he was included in the "unable to trust bunch," so pretty much anything he would have said to me concerning our past break up should have fallen on deaf ears. He began asking me specific questions surrounding my accusations against him. I would point to this and that, and other things that happened, and before I knew it, *he pitched a curve ball...*

He had absolutely no knowledge of this person telling me (lies) about "their relationship." He didn't deny the fact they had gone out, but what I had believed for over twenty years was not that he dated other people, but that he kept cheating on me behind my back with this person. We both dated other people during the times we broke up, and always ended up getting back together. We both took each other for granted in our youth. I never told him about what was being said to me or how this person would taunt and humiliate me publicly. *For whatever reason, I believed this person's lies, even though they had absolutely no credibility.* They were always insanely jealous of me, and at every turn the devil used this person to do his job, ultimately keeping us torn apart.

As Mike began to explain his side of the story something happened deep within my spirit and soul. He had never been given the opportunity to explain his side of the story prior to me leaving in June of 1993. My ears were supernaturally opened up, and the Holy Spirit validated in my inner man, my heart, what Mike was telling me was *true*. Every bit of it was true, and I knew that God was indeed assuring me, he wasn't making any of it up. For the very first time ever in my life, I believed that *he really did love me* all those years ago! The truth of the matter is I believed Satan's lies. Mike never rejected me for anybody else, I just didn't know it!

In an instant, quicker than I could have snapped my finger, my soul was awakened from the grave. God's light fiercely pierced my darkness. I had an unexplainable, instantaneous joy bubbling up out of me. It came from the inside out, and there wasn't anything I could do to stop it, or try to hide it. It was like a spring of water with continual movement creating a surge of nonstop joy. Buckets of joy, multiplied over and over kept surging within me. I began crying and laughing as I was trying to figure out what had just happened to me. This bubbly-joy experience continued for days, nonstop, at a supernatural level.

What happened to me truly is a phenomenon. It's so difficult to describe in our limited vocabulary. Soon after, I began hearing lyrics to songs and melodies as if they had just come alive inside me. I was more in tune with other people and my surroundings. Things that once appeared dead to me were now living and breathing instruments of pleasure to my soul. It's one of the most complex things to describe, and one of the most amazing things that God has ever done for me.

This major breakthrough in my life didn't help Mike in his time of need. He was still in the same condition he had been in, which was critical. Once the truth was revealed it hit us hard. We both realized how devastating this was. I believed for all those years that the one and only true love of my life had rejected me. From his perspective, it wasn't fair at all to him. His first love left him one day without warning or explanation. We had lost over twenty years of our lives, and went on to discover that we both had empty voids that no one else could ever fill. *All because I believed a lie, we both were crushed.* He never understood why I left. I never told him.

He did his best to be happy for me, because I had just become the most joyful woman in the world. He struggled with this new found information, and I really felt bad for him. Here I was, believing God to move on his behalf, and give him back his mind. Yet day after day, I couldn't help but be chipper and happy. I hadn't ever felt that way before, and there was nothing I could do to keep it hidden.

Believing this lie from the devil kept me *BOUND* for over twenty years. The course of my life was completely altered, and it was all based on what I believed to be true. During my entire adult life, the devil worked hard to create all kinds of smoke and mirrors, making good look bad, and bad look good. Do you know what I mean? Most of my former relationships were dysfunctional, not all were abusive, but many were.

It's true that our relationship was tested from time to time as kids, but we always ended up making up and moved on. The major component of permanent damage done to my heart from our breakup when I left him in 1993 was an issue of trust. The devil was sure to send spirits of rejection, abandonment, and despair into my life due to the significant pain of loss I experienced. No human being can heal that kind of wound.

Remember the true biblical account of the daughter of Abraham, who was tormented by an evil spirit of infirmity, whom the devil kept in bondage eighteen years?

Luke 13: 11, 16 (KJV)

[11] And, behold, there was a woman which had a spirit of infirmity eighteen years, and was bowed together, and could in no wise lift up herself.

[16] And ought not this woman, being a daughter of Abraham, whom Satan hath bound, lo, these eighteen years, be loosed from this bond on the Sabbath day?

Well, I can relate! I, too, am a daughter of Abraham, with rights and privileges through my personal relationship with God the Father through His Son, Jesus Christ. If people in Bible history days could be hoodwinked by Satan, why would we be any different? I could in no wise have lifted myself up either. It's only by God's grace that He *on purpose* reached down from Heaven, lifted me up, and made a very bad wrong right. He gave me truth with the ability to *receive and know* it to be true. *God truly loves justice!*

The four Scriptures

As Mike and I would spend time on the phone, he would share how he was stuck on the bathroom floor, not showering or eating right for days without number. My heart was in a state of urgency; I knew he was right on death's doorstep. The thoughts he expressed didn't show any real signs of improvement. As a matter of fact, some days were so dark; it was as if his life was being held together by a very tiny thread of hope. On a daily basis, I had to give him great big doses of encouragement, even though he was hesitant or resistant; most of the time it was as if my words just bounced right back to me. My faith and hope was deep within me, based on God's faithfulness and mercy. Determined to not give up on him, I couldn't pay any attention to the natural circumstances.

I gave Mike some instructions for a biblical prescription to get control of his mind. I know he must have thought I was crazy. We as kids never learned anything about praying in the Spirit or speaking God's Word over our lives to gain victory. That was all foreign to him. I asked him if he had a Bible. He said he did, so I asked him to get a pen and paper to write down four passages of Scripture. The medicine he needed most was God's Holy Word containing divine healing. No one in the natural could have ever provided what only God Himself was about to give him. He needed supernatural help, because he was in a spiritual battle for his soul. His very life was almost stolen from him prematurely.

The prescription was to read those four passages at least several times a day out loud. Clearly in the beginning, he didn't understand the concept of speaking the Word of God out loud. He said because it had been so long since I had asked him to do something, he would consent even though he didn't see the value in it. I further explained, even if he didn't understand what the Scriptures meant it was okay, because the Word of God is anointed and contains power within itself. If he would do as I said,

I knew the Word would begin to go to work, and God would manifest His power in Mike's mind through the working of the Holy Spirit. The four Scriptures I asked him to confess out loud were Second Timothy 1:7, Titus 2:8a, Isaiah 26:3 and Psalm 23:3.

Battle cries for mercy

On a nonstop basis, I was pleading before God's throne of grace, pleading for mercy over Mike's soul. I would be up early and stay awake late. Praying all hours of the night, I'd find myself carrying this heavy burden that God would save him, and heal his mind. This went on for days. At times he would be on an emotional roller coaster. It was part of my job to help keep his feelings in check. I didn't want him to become too emotional about anything, and the fact I made contact with him could have destroyed him if I weren't careful.

Our "safe" boundaries were constantly being monitored and reinforced. We both knew it would be dangerous to have a deep conversation about ourselves or our feelings. Many times over, I wouldn't allow any of my feelings to surface. I knew the truth that I still loved him, and feeling his pain was devastating to me, but there was no way I could have shown any signs of emotion. My job was laser focused to keep him moving closer to Jesus, so he could get back on his feet.

Frequently he would tell me that what he was going through was so unfair. His life was dark, very dark. It was evident; he had absolutely no hope of any kind of ever getting through this tragic time. I continued to assure him that God loved him and was with him, that God had a good plan for his life, and for him to look to Jesus for the strength and comfort he desperately needed.

How can this be?

Shortly after these first few days that we had contact over the telephone, after the truth had been revealed about our breakup, God did something else in my life that came unexpectedly. On January 8, 2015, I had a mini vision. While standing in an alter type setting, I saw Mike facing me, he was on the left, and I was on the right. I was wearing a beautiful long gown. In an instant, the Lord revealed to me that Mike and I would be married. There was an "inner witness" on the inside, the Holy Spirit, who confirmed what He had just shown me was indeed the truth about my future. It's extremely difficult to explain, but I had such peace even while my heart was so heavily burdened for Mike's recovery.

Mike repeatedly would tell me the same things over and over, that it was so unfair what he was experiencing. He seemed paralyzed, and beyond all hope in the natural. I knew he couldn't make sense of much of anything that I would say, especially when I would try to comfort him with Scripture or prayer. His mind in the natural realm seemed unrepairable. Time seemed to stand still with very little progress. For many days there weren't any outward signs of any inward changes. It was as though he was barely alive, taking one breath at a time; his life seemed to be quickly vanishing.

I called my best girlfriend to share with her what God had just showed me, and she (in her wisdom) cautioned me not to share any of these things I saw in the Spirit with Mike; at least not then. He was too fragile, and the last thing he needed was someone he once loved so deeply to relay this kind of information to him, and delay his healing through selfishness. I'm so thankful for her; she always has been a great sounding board, and provides excellent counsel. It was decided that I wouldn't tell any of this to Mike until the time was right. There was just this one thing I pondered over and over in my mind besides, "How can this be?" I simply couldn't understand why he was on the left. In traditional wedding ceremonies, I always saw the bride on the left, and the groom on the right. It was odd to see, but in due time the revelation with the interpretation would come.

Prophetic repentance, come forth

On January 13, 2015, the Lord began speaking to me about Mike's repentance, and I was impressed in my heart to record some very significant events in my journal concerning Mike's battle. I said these things out loud, and then recorded how I was led to make a declaration over Mike's life. I wrote:

"Deep calleth unto deep. I'm a prophetic voice in the wilderness crying, Repent! Repent! Repent! So that you may Rejoice! Rejoice! Rejoice!" (I had been watching one of my favorite ministers who taught on the Spirit of seeing and knowing. It's when the Holy Spirit operates through a person prophetically). That same day I had prayed, "Father, please fine tune my hearing and my seeing, so that I may walk in the fullness of the Spirit of seeing and knowing. It's what I feed on; that's what I become. Let me walk and feed on these truths in Jesus' Name, and minster out of my overflow for Your glory. My protection is automatic, like an automatic weapon, equally important in all my spiritual armor; filled in my heart and mouth equals praise and thanksgiving unto My God. For you, Oh Lord, do only wondrous things. Your love has no measure. Your mercy is boundless. Your heartbeat is one with mine. I love you, Father God. Thank you, Jesus, for saving me. I love you, Lord. Thank you, Holy Spirit, You lead and guide me with Your eye into all Truth. You show me things to come. You remind me of things Jesus has spoken to my heart, and You teach me all things. Thank you, Lord Jesus."

It was never disclosed to Mike that the Lord led me to pray in such a way for him. Knowing it would come across judgmental or critical, I abstained from telling him that God wanted him to repent.

Immediately after this prayer and declaration, things began developing at rapid speed. Mike and I had been talking for hours at a time on the telephone, and texting when possible. Then the unbelievable was about to unfold. My emotions were on overload. I knew in my heart that I had always loved Mike, but up until this point I had been extremely successful in concealing my love for him. *There was absolutely no way humanly possible that I could've told him how I felt, but then, it happened...*

A small window opened up, it's very hard to describe. We were texting one morning, and he seemed to be doing extremely better and gaining strength. He had come so far along from a place of tragedy, pain, suffering, loss and mental instability. We would take breaks when needed if our conversations seemed to get too emotional. He was gaining peace, hope, contentment and happiness. He had gone from being almost incompetent to being able to carry on a normal conversation with me. *What I witnessed God doing in Mike's life was truly miraculous, especially in such a short period of time!*

That small window of opportunity was undeniable, and it made me extremely nervous! Time was ticking, and just as fast as that "window" appeared, it slowly started to dissipate. There was a gentle nudge in my heart, deep within my spirit, to take a step of faith. With my heart racing and super sweaty palms, in the spur of a moment, I did the unimaginable. I did exactly *opposite* of what I told myself not to do. I texted him those three unforgettable words, *"I love you,"* and before I could think about any potential consequences, I hit "send."

Believe me when I say he never saw that coming! Deep down I had an unquenchable desire to share that truth with him, knowing if I failed to keep it a secret from him much longer it would be wrong. That window opened up in front of me – *Supernaturally!* It was there, carved out for that specific moment in time, and it was precisely the right moment he needed to know the truth.

On January 15, 2015, Mike said he wanted to share all his secrets of everything and anything he could think of, that may potentially hurt me down the road, if I were to find out about certain things from his past. He also said he wanted to openly ask God for forgiveness, to repent, and then also ask me for forgiveness. One day later, he did just that. *It was so powerful!* He made a list of items to disclose, and as I sat on the floor listening to his heart, I was beyond speechless. It was obvious to me, and I knew in my heart, he truly was "sorrowful with repentance." God moved quickly on his behalf, so that Mike could be free and rejoice!

The fact that someone would care enough about my feelings to discuss hidden secrets, and remove the potential harm that could lie ahead if I heard rumors about his past, boggled my mind. It was very difficult to wrap my mind around this. In the end, after the painful confession with repentance for Mike concluded, it was so liberating for him, and I knew from that day forward, we would have no more secrets. From that day until now, our love for one another has been unshakable. To this very day we still practice "no secrets."

What kind of amazing does someone have to be to disclose shameful and hurtful things openly, and then ask God and me to forgive him? That's a broken vessel, one fit for the Kingdom of God; it exemplifies both humility and strength. It's difficult to describe the new depth of our love for each other after this took place. We were given a brand new level of confidence in one another, to believe in our love once again; we now have complete trust, openness and transparency.

It was then that I could better understand why the Lord had me intercede for Mike's repentance; it moved him one step closer to Jesus and another step closer toward his total deliverance from the hand of Satan. To hear him rejoicing after everything was out in the open was *priceless*.

The curse has been broken!

What a glorious testimony unto our God! He is always faithful to forgive us, and cleanse us from all our unrighteousness (see First John 1:9). All we have to do is repent, ask for, and then receive God's forgiveness. Jesus is the Peace Giver, the Way Maker, the Omnipotent all powerful, amazingly-wonderful God. Wow!

In addition to all that he disclosed that day, sometime later Mike shared with me how he repented to the Lord for leaving me when we were just kids, when he went into the Marine Corps. He said after he repented he sensed the curse of us always being apart had finally been broken off our lives.

Soon it would be revealed that the awful curse that Satan used to torment us, the curse of being torn apart, had finally been destroyed, and good things, incredibly-amazing things were right around the corner!

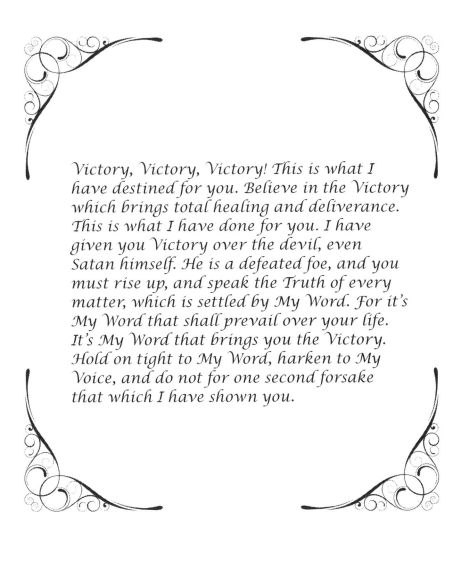

Victory, Victory, Victory! This is what I have destined for you. Believe in the Victory which brings total healing and deliverance. This is what I have done for you. I have given you Victory over the devil, even Satan himself. He is a defeated foe, and you must rise up, and speak the Truth of every matter, which is settled by My Word. For it's My Word that shall prevail over your life. It's My Word that brings you the Victory. Hold on tight to My Word, harken to My Voice, and do not for one second forsake that which I have shown you.

Chapter Nine

EXCEEDINGLY ABOVE

It always amazes me how sometimes God speaks to us, and we may not even understand what it means in its entirety when spoken. God's Word never grows old and is multidimensional. He can speak confirming words or sometimes a brand new word, maybe one we've never heard before. Initially on the surface, it may have little or no real significant meaning. Often as time progresses, He unveils more truth about the things He has said. I love it when that happens. We get to see pieces of the handiwork of God woven throughout our lives; turning it into a beautiful masterpiece by our Maker.

For example, back around springtime 2012, the Lord gave me a vision. I saw myself standing on a large battlefield. Jesus was standing in front of me facing toward me. In my peripheral vision I could see dead bodies lying all across this field. Jesus wanted me to keep my focus on Him. He didn't want me to look to my right or to my left. He wanted my eyes fully stayed on Him. He also wanted me to take steps forward. He assured me that He would lead me to anyone that was on the battlefield that needed my help. I also saw an infirmary in the background, behind the battlefield. The picture I drew from the infirmary was one who was severely injured, barely alive, and in a sense being operated on, but their face wasn't visible. All the while I was instructed to just keep my eyes upon Jesus. At the end of the vision, He assured me if I would only maintain my focus on Him, and Him only *that even I would be amazed at who was back in the infirmary,* and their life would be saved. At that time, I concluded from the vision that it would only be revealed to me one day in Heaven, whose life it was that I saw in the infirmary that God would use me to help save.

It wasn't until Mike came through that spiritual operating table, and the Holy Spirit was able to do the work He needed to do, that I was able to connect the dots, and see that the vision from the Lord in 2012 came to pass in my life in 2015. God used me, a broken vessel, who kept her eyes upon Jesus to help save Mike's life. What's so amazing now to me was the timing of the vision. You see, I was married to someone else at the time God gave me that vision. Isn't that funny how God knew exactly what was needed, and just at the right time?

In addition to that, I had yet another vision concerning Mike later that same year in December 2012. While in my living room sitting on the sofa, out of nowhere it came. I hadn't thought about Mike in a while, I was dealing with my own issues at the time, and was going through a difficult situation. Mike and I never had any communication in over twenty years. I actually had forgotten all about this particular vision concerning him when we first started talking through Facebook in December of 2014.

What I saw in this second vision was frightening. It was very satanic and gothic. It was something so strong that as I was in the Spirit, I felt as though it was going to pull me right in with it. It was devilish and scary, but this is what seemed so frightful to me: At the time of the vision, I was Spirit filled and loved Jesus. I was living for the Lord, but what I saw that had a hold on Mike was *EXTREMELY* pleasurable to the senses. How in the world can something so deadly seem so pleasurable to the senses?

The soul of man is Satan's playground. Our soul is comprised of our mind, will and emotions. We are a three part being. Perhaps some of you may have heard it said that we are a spirit being, we possess a soul, and live in a body. It's through our senses, soul, and physical body that Satan comes to steal, kill and destroy. If he can successfully entice people through their soul, he can then master their mind and control their will, and ultimately dominate their flesh.

I was extremely concerned at that time for Mike's life, for I saw his life hanging in a balance. It was so disturbing that I sent him a message through Facebook trying to warn him. I didn't really want to message him back in 2012. I didn't know anything at all about his life; if he was single or married; or if he would even take the time to read a message from me or not. The vision concerning him was horrific and unimaginable. The Lord was leading me to give the message to him as a wakeup call. I sent Mike the message below, and never received a response.

December 28, 2012

"Dear Mike, I am writing with only pure intentions, if you are married or in a relationship, I am not trying to divide your home or family, so please forgive me. I would never try to cause anyone grief or sadness, but I saw someone's life near and dear to my heart, hanging in a balance. It's not easy for me to type this; equally, it may not be easily received. Either way, I want you to know that God loves you, and He has a plan and purpose for your life. Seeds of His love have been planted in you, and He simply wanted you to know He sees and knows you, and His love is the only force that compels me to share His Good News."

This is such a critical piece of my story. Mike had never responded to that message. I just assumed he read it, and probably deleted it since it was from me. According to him, he never got the message when it was originally sent. He said that it wasn't until he hit the "send" button to tell me that he wasn't going to accept my friend's request, that then my original message from December 28, 2012, appeared in his dialogue box. Once he saw that I had tried to reach out to him prior to this difficult time in his life, something on the inside of him led him to believe that I was there not to hurt him, but that I really did care. I only had pure intentions when I sent him that friend's request, but how could he have known that?

He claimed at the time when he first read that old message from December 2012, he had no idea what it meant or what it was about. As time went on it became real clear. The bondage he was buried in was so deep and dark that Satan, the enemy of his soul, was fighting every inch of the way trying to steal, kill and destroy him, and ultimately bring Mike to a premature death.

Thank God for the Holy Ghost! *THANK GOD FOR THE HOLY GHOST!* He is alive! He shows us things to come. There is a God in Heaven who loves us! He is the One and only true living God, and He is alive today and forevermore!

Out of darkness, into the Light

I'm so grateful, so thankful unto the Lord for sending help to me along my path during various times of need. Reflecting back, it seems as though many of the greatest trials of my life led me to draw closer and go deeper into my relationship with my heavenly Father. At times, He used some people along the way to help point me back to Him.

On October 12, 2014, I was praying about where I was to move to. I shared with a Pastor and his wife that I was uncertain about where God was leading me. They ministered to me for a while, and then prayed with me. Then all of a sudden, the Pastor said that God was speaking to me, and I was told to *go back to my first love*. At the time, I took it that my first love meant a place to live, not a person. Initially I had the wrong interpretation. The Lord put my feet on the right course, and looking back now, I see how God planted words to confirm His plan, and help light my path along the way.

In early November of 2014, I received a Happy Birthday wish from an acquaintance through Facebook, who told me the origin of my first and middle name, and what they meant. The essence of what they conveyed was my name meant "a good spear." They likened it to being a weapon that a seasoned warrior can count on. Then they prophetically wrote, "You are going to do the job. Accomplish the call that God has ordained for your life. You are a dangerous woman to the kingdom of darkness." I had no idea what that meant at the time, or how significant those prophetic words were. I never even received a message from that person before, and they knew very little about me!

Then on January 2, 2015, someone different sent me yet another message, which said that God was working something *"beautiful"* in my life, and that I just needed to have a little patience. I can tell you at the moment when I read that message, it practically bounced right off of me. Something deep within wanted to believe it, but there was so much sadness and depression that had brought me to a place of accepting a life filled with hopelessness. The person that sent that message to me also had very little knowledge about my life, and lives in another country! How could they have known that, except by the revelation knowledge through the ministry of the Holy Spirit?

These messages that God was trying to convey to me to give me hope came from the most uncommon of places, and at times when natural circumstances screamed otherwise. These random messages did not come from people who had intimate knowledge about me. They had absolutely no clue what was really going on inside my head, nor did these people have any substantial knowledge about my past or what then was my present.

One day while I was praying in the Spirit, faith had risen in my heart, and I got into agreement with what God had been trying to convince me of. I declared out loud for the very first time ever that my life was beautiful, and I earnestly thanked the Lord that He made my life beautiful. Believe me, there was nothing beautiful that I could see at the time, but faith rose up in my heart, and I acted upon my faith in what God had said about me.

Little did I know at the time, how real the phase from Ecclesiastes truly was; that God *"makes all things beautiful in His time,"* and it would soon come to pass in my own life. It wasn't until a few months later, when all the things that I received from the Lord began making more sense, and then I could begin to see the bigger picture.

Others, many others, knowingly or unknowingly were used against me in strong opposition to try to steal God's plan and purposes away from me. Regardless, I know that I know; God's hand has been upon my life. His Voice is like deep rushing waters, so powerful, and it carries far more weight than the enemies I face. It is He who gives me breath, and I am still standing with no fear of the faces of man.

Love vs. Law

Once during a very difficult and painful situation in my life, I was struggling whether or not to cover up or expose someone's sin, which if exposed at the time could have gotten them expelled from a ministerial school. Not only were they daily sinning against God, themselves and me, but sadly they lived in great denial concerning their behavior and actions. The devil had gained entrance into this person's life, and was able to get them way off track from the call of God on their life.

During this much confusing time, I was having lunch one day with a Spirit filled lady who pastored a church. She had a trustworthy reputation, and I believed she could provide the wisdom I desperately needed. I confided in her concerning some of the things that I had been going through to get some godly counsel.

Although I already knew from the Lord He didn't want me to run away from this heartbreaking experience or expose this person's sin, I still struggled on so many emotional levels. That day she gave me some excellent advice, and encouraged me to stay strong, to stay connected to the Lord, and not give place to those pain-filled deceitful thoughts that ceaselessly tormented me.

From the time she had counseled me, within a little more than one year that person chose to abandon my life, and the major torments finally ceased. I still had a long period of recovery from emotional pain to deal with, but the primary issues causing the heartache weren't as visible.

Surprisingly it was a relief to me once they left, even though I was alone and felt rejected. After all, we had spent time together, so there was a soul tie that I needed to deal with. There was however, a strong knowing in the depth of my heart it was for the best.

The Lord spoke to me through a dream concerning this person several months before they left. In the dream were four demons, two were directly affecting me, and the other two were in the background, which appeared to be waiting to exercise punishment. They didn't look good to say the least, but the Lord never gave me the full interpretation of the other two that were in the background. I only knew in part, specifically about the two demons that were being used against me. The leader of the group was trying to keep me bound from preaching the Gospel. The second mini demon was a little "annoyance" who continually mocked God. As it mocked God, the strength it once had was becoming less and less effective.

What's relevant here that I want to point out is the person who provided godly wisdom and counsel never assessed her judgment, for the person who was living in habitual sin, nor toward me. She only spoke the truth about what the Bible said, and encouraged me with Scripture to support her counsel. I was in a very dark place, and found myself looking frantically for answers. I felt as if I could trust no one with what I was sharing with her. It was so disturbing, but I didn't want to expose this person's sin publicly either.

It wasn't an easy battle as my soul was under constant attack with seemingly little or no break. I found great comfort in her words. *Her words were filled with Grace.* She ministered *life* to me that day; she didn't criticize, pass judgment or look down on me. Do you understand there is a vast difference between Grace and Law, especially in this particular case?

Law when used as a weapon apart from God's love births judgment. Hypocrites judge, and then live any ole sloppy way they want to while preaching at you. Sometimes you may hear some good sounding advice, including quotes from Scripture, but the whole while they make you feel like they are beating you over the head with their Bible (even though they themselves may have no real victory over sin in their life).

Grace ministered to us through God's love is *ALWAYS* given for deliverance. Grace doesn't keep a person in bondage; it provides the power needed to free us from all bondages. Grace provides power to overcome sin and the devil. Grace brings life, liberty and freedom. Law keeps man under. Grace is what God gives. Man apart from God, gives humanistic approach with judgment. That's what living under the Law will do for religious folks. They just can't help themselves, and offer up what they think is their "spiritual" yet seemingly empty advice. It's of no value, and only breeds contention and rebellion toward God and people.

The person who helped me in my time of need exercised Love, not Law; she pointed me to the Spirit of Truth, the Word of God, and the Spirit of Grace. She gave me exactly what I needed to do warfare against the devil, who was my real enemy. The person who hurt me in the process was never really my enemy. The devil just worked through that person to try to get me to back down from pursuing the call of God on my life. She surrounded me with faith and love, and withheld any criticizing judgment from the equation. She was a true reflection of Jesus to me that day. She is a mighty warrior, greatly used by God, and humbly serves the Lord with her whole heart.

Another thing to be said about ministering to others when giving godly counsel; it's so important to remember people who are hurting are fragile. It's not the time or place to point fingers. If a man is overboard, would you throw him a rock or a life vest?

After this person who had been secretly living in sin had abandoned me, I sent the lady I had confided in about the situation a text message and discreetly asked for prayer. I didn't want people in my business. Sharing all the private details about this situation has never publicly been discussed, nor will it ever be. My heart was broken because of unfaithfulness and sin, but in the end, my heart was broken more for their need of salvation and repentance.

This person had once claimed to be a child of God. They had backslidden so bad that their mind became inhabited with strongholds from the devil, and the enemy began calling all the shots in this person's life. I had earnestly prayed for this person's soul, that the Lord would be merciful, and bring them back to Him. After that prayer, I heard the Lord say to me to not look back (with regret). He reminded me of the true account in the Bible referencing the passage about Lot's wife. He instructed me to not look back, ever.

One final note about the lady who kept pointing me to Jesus in those really hard times; her reply to my text requesting prayer when the person had left me needs to be shared. It really encouraged and strengthened my heart. During that difficult time I wondered how I could ever go on. I held onto her words for days, months, and now some years after. Her reply said, "When the smoke clears and the dust settles, I see you standing in your victory." What she did for me was priceless. She didn't criticize, question, bring conviction or shame, she simply encouraged me to stay strong in the Lord, and in the power of His might.

That life lesson of true godly ministry became so evident to me that day. Because I had been shown the way of God's love, not judgment, it helped point me back to my true source of strength, and taught me how I need to minister to people today. It helps immensely to realize if we seize moments that God gives us to share His love, it should be about Him, not us. Our words and actions should demonstrate humility, not criticism. I was so fragile at the time she ministered to me. I was extremely broken, and needed God's grace, mercy, and love, not Law.

The prophetic laugh

Once while going out on a date something very unusual happened to me. This was in fact the last person I had dated that led me to conclude I really had no business dating anyone, that it was useless. While on this particular date, I had a *prophetic laugh*. I didn't even know that anything like this existed at the time, nor did I have the interpretation right away. The revelation with the interpretation was kept hidden from me for more than one year!

On the first date, I was asked probably one of the rudest questions I had ever been faced with before. It blindsided me, I never saw it coming. We had just been seated at a really nice, upscale restaurant with people all around us, and without warning the first question that popped out of his mouth was, "Have you ever been sexually abused in any of your past relationships?" Wow! I was shocked to say the least. Dumbfounded by this inappropriate question from someone I barely knew, I quickly hushed him, and said we should talk about that later. We never did. How embarrassing!

As the evening was coming to an end, it was decided that ice cream sounded pretty good. While eating ice cream, we were sitting down, and I mentioned a story concerning my best girlfriend. While I was talking, something extremely unusual began happening to me. It's probably one of the most unbelievable things I've ever witnessed in my life. This uncontrollable, hysterical laugh hit me like there was no tomorrow. I mean, it went on and on and on. For at least a solid five minutes or longer, I had no control over this laugh. It was so deep in my belly it tickled! It tickled my belly so much, and the more I would laugh, the more it would make me laugh. I couldn't make it stop. Are you able to picture this? It was one of the craziest things I have ever experienced.

To provide a brief description of myself, I am an extreme opposite of a sanguine. I can be witty or funny, but it's usually not on purpose. I am definitely not the life of any party trying to draw unnecessary attention to myself. Being so serious, perhaps you can imagine how this may have made me feel. I was embarrassed, and tried to pull myself together. It was nonsense to me to be crying with extreme laughter as my eyes were filled with tears, and for reasons I didn't understand at the time. There was just no controlling or stopping it.

Are you able to see more clearly now that Satan is the master deceiver who loves to produce counterfeits to God's authentic originals? He wants to keep us from the plans and purposes that were created for us even before the foundations of the world. The devil will purposefully and methodically "set up" circumstances to make things look like they are as good as they will ever get. Satan's plan is for us to compromise and settle. In the process, we lose all hope with constant feelings of defeat, and loss of purpose. Finally, we stop pursuing our dreams. *His traps always are baited by things we desire most, and are used to keep us from God's best.*

Counterfeits can be easily recognized, because they come in packages laced with disappointment and uneasiness. Many times you sense a heaviness produced by your intuition and inner man, which are telling you that you're settling.

According to the Power at work in us

The Lord desires for us to seek His face, to study His Word, and to develop our spirits to have eyes to see, and ears to hear His Voice, the Spirit of Truth. When we begin to seek the Lord with our whole heart, He will do for us what we cannot do ourselves. He will begin the process of changing and molding us into His image from the inside out. He changes us little by little as we go from glory to glory.

As children of God, we can then be led by the Spirit of God. We can overcome Satan, the world, and our flesh to live a victorious life of freedom from the fear of death, and bondage to man. Satan is our enemy, and he uses mankind to influence this world system. If we aren't on guard, we can fall prey right into the enemy's traps and get hoodwinked. Knowing who you are in Christ, renewing your mind to the Word of God, and then acting upon it are all equally imperative to live a successful life, and help you avoid those hidden traps. It won't guarantee a life absent of problems, but it will guarantee you to conquer and overcome in the face of adversity.

The bottom line is regardless of our past, if it was a poor choice on our part or we were violated that brought us pain, shame or regret; God loves you and me, and wants to bring blessings into our lives. I am His child, and He has stood with me when many others wouldn't during those painful times of trial and tribulation. He knows the desires of our hearts. He knows every detail of our lives. Since I was twelve years old, I have claimed *Psalm 37:4* as my favorite verse. It says, *"If we delight ourselves in the Lord, He will give us the desires of our hearts."*

Now that verse is more alive in me than ever! It's taken on a whole new meaning with a deeper reality in my life. I am not only delighting myself in the Lord, pursuing Him passionately, but He truly has over abundantly, supernaturally, over exceedingly, beyond my wildest dreams, made His Word good in my life. He performs on my behalf, and manifests Himself daily to me. Just because He can! Just because He is good! Just because He is the One and only true living God, and just because He loves me! God is a giver! He gives and *MAKES* a way where there seems to be no way!

Your eyes have been unveiled. The Truth about My love for you has been revealed. The walls of rejection that surrounded you were built only for your protection; to bring you back to life from the dead. You are a living, breathing testament that these dead dry bones can indeed live. Run, Run, Run today; for victory has been placed into your hands.

Behold, you used to be like the world.

You looked like the world.

You dressed like the world.

You behaved like the world.

People used to judge and criticize you then.

Today you are My child. I delight over you with singing and joy. You have chosen Me over the temporary pleasures of the world. I hold you up with My right hand of Righteousness.

I AM knows your name. I am that I AM. I love you, cherish you, and when others falsely accuse or rise up against you, Remember: MY VICTORY IS YOUR VICTORY!

Chapter Ten

BLESSED BEYOND MEASURE

The anticipation of seeing Mike face to face after twenty-one and a half years was equally exciting and nerve-racking. We had been promising each other absolutely no kissing at the airport (where we agreed to meet), and wouldn't kiss at all until the right time for that matter. Obviously neither of us knew what the other person would look like after twenty-one and a half years of aging, but I was pretty sure I'd still think he was the most handsome, gorgeous man in the world, and might be tempted to kiss him! As time drew near for our reunion, I had an overwhelming amount of butterflies in my stomach.

Mike helped prepare me as much as possible over the telephone, as I was concerned I might wind up sitting on the airplane, and forget what to do next. Sounds a bit crazy I know, but I was *so nervous!* He gave me helpful hints on how to breathe deeply, so I wouldn't pass out from being filled with too much excitement or anxiety.

This was one of the hardest things I had ever done. I was just about to see the man of my dreams, the one man I truly loved without measure. How could any of this even happen in such a short period of time? What will people think? Will I even care? Does it even matter? This particular airport was always such a grim place for us. Those old memories soon crept up as

I could recall countless "good-byes" at this very airport while he was in the Marine Corps.

My plane had just landed; my heartbeat was pounding uncontrollably as reality was sinking in fast. I was telling myself to put one foot in front of the other and keep walking. This was our special time. This was the beginning of a brand new beginning of possibilities for us. This is what we wanted, we wanted to be together. We were as ready as we would ever be to see one another, face to face and nose to nose.

As I left the plane that day and began walking through that familiar airport, they were playing sad, sappy 80's music. I thought, *"Are you kidding me?"* It was almost as if they had inside information that we planned to meet, and at the precise moments leading up to us reuniting, they knew exactly what songs to play. They played those heart-wrenching songs that used to tear us to pieces while we were apart as kids. It was as if all the music had been preselected just for us.

I saw Mike standing in the far off distance awaiting my arrival as I walked down the long hallway. I didn't have my glasses on so he was fuzzy for most of the time. Then as I walked closer and closer toward him, I had to tell myself to just keep breathing, one deep breath at a time. It wasn't until I was just a few feet away I then could get a close up look at his handsome face!

Without saying a word, he pulled me toward him, and held me tightly in his arms. It was an extremely emotional time for us both. We never spoke a word during this unforgettable embrace. Tears were flowing down his cheeks, and touching my face like a waterfall. He couldn't stop sobbing, not for one minute during this time. My emotions were all over the place, too. I was resisting the temptation of crying, although my feelings were very hard to contain. This may sound silly, but I didn't want my makeup to start running. I wanted him to think I was beautiful. It had been a really long time, and I wanted him to remember how I looked for him on that special day. I had a reason to get all dolled up, and didn't want to ruin it!

It's safe to assume, had it not of been for having to pick up my luggage in the baggage claim area, most likely we may have been there in that same spot much longer. We had to go down a ways to the carousel, and pick up my one bag that I checked in. While I didn't time how long our embrace was, this is only an estimate, I am guessing it was for twenty-five to thirty minutes. The airport staff was just about to take my luggage to the lost and found, since I hadn't been there to claim it.

Our most memorable Valentine's Day

It was our first date out on the town. I bought a new dress, and pair of black leather boots to go out for dinner. Mike said he was taking me out for Valentine's Day, and I wanted to look my best for him. The weather was pretty bad that evening, it was snowing and freezing cold outside. I had just left eighty degree weather to see him, and was not prepared for the low temperature chill factor. He originally planned to take me out to see a movie, and eat dinner at a restaurant nearby the movie theater. It was decided that he was going to take me to a closer restaurant in town, and skip the movie due to the drifting snow.

Without a dinner reservation, we walked in to one of the nicest restaurants in town, had no wait time although they were extremely busy, and got seated in a private area away from the main crowd. We couldn't have planned it out that way. We got to spend quality time together with uninterrupted conversation, and were simply enjoying each other's company without distractions from other people. The food was prepared perfectly, and we had excellent service. We were able to enjoy the ambiance, and it definitely was one of the most romantic evenings of my life!

As we left the restaurant, Mike never told me where we were going as he drove around town. He kept it a surprise. I hadn't been to this certain part of town since we were kids. The surroundings looked somewhat familiar, but I still had no idea what he was up to.

There was a very familiar landmark to my right. Then it hit me! He was taking me to the place we used to park as kids! It was our special place. He pulled off to the side of the road, and began talking to me about his desire of getting things right with God. He asked if we could pray, repent, and ask God to forgive us for the things we had done outside of God's will, while we were just two young, crazy kids in love. During this prayer, Mike asked God if He would take that place we once held special in our hearts, and to sanctify it, making it clean and holy, so that it could be a new place of dedication and consecration unto the Lord. Once he prayed that prayer, the blessings came pouring down!

That night Mike spoke to me out of the very depth of his heart and soul telling me what I meant to him, and how thankful he was to be with me again. He is the manliest man I have ever known. The fact that he has such a deep love for me, and is enough of a man to share his true feelings without holding anything back, makes me feels valuable, cherished and loved.

He put a lot of thought into his words and prayer that night. It wasn't something he found on the internet or just pulled out of thin air. I believe God inspired him to give him the right words at the right time. After he poured out his heart to me, and shared all the ways he loved me, would take care of me, and how he desired for God to make him into the man that I deserved to have; he then proceeded to ask that very special question. *You know the question!* That one question I heard him ask three other times before.

While asking me to marry him and be his wife, he handed me a small box. When I opened the box, it lit up with a tiny little light. Inside was the most beautiful diamond ring I had ever seen. He picked it out especially for me. It was stunning and breathtaking. This moment in time was absolutely incredible, and if I could have had just *one wish* that evening, *I would have wished for that night to never end.*

Our lives had been violently torn apart, but now our friendship had been restored, and this time when he proposed I knew, that I knew, that I knew… *he really loved me!* It was undeniable. I believed in all my heart that this was part of God's perfect plan for us to come back together, and of course, I said, "YES!"

Our first day of Forever!

The day finally came, and the countdown was over. The atmosphere was filled with much anticipation and excitement! We exchanged our vows at a lovely church, and had a wonderful man of God as our minister to perform our wedding ceremony. We had been practicing safe boundaries to avoid tarnishing what God wanted to bless us with: Blessings beyond measure in our marriage.

We mutually agreed upfront that we wouldn't kiss on the lips when the preacher would say, "You may now kiss your bride." The time came to put into play what we had practiced and rehearsed; when the minister said to Mike that he could kiss his bride, Mike kissed me on the cheek. Mike was told he didn't follow very good instructions, and needed to give me a *real* kiss. To everyone's surprise, Mike announced that we had waited all that time and hadn't kissed, and the first time he was going to kiss me was going to be in the privacy of our own place with no onlookers. Let me just say this to put your mind at ease; it was definitely worth the wait!

In writing our wedding vows, we both earnestly prayed to seek God's will, and wrote vows that would forever keep our hearts united as one in Christ. We held nothing back; we both were transparent before God, and were completely vulnerable with each other. I truly believe because we honored God to the best of our ability, we now have a transcendent love, genuine friendship, complete trust, and no secrets. We are filled with joy unspeakable as God has blessed us, and gave us *Our first day of Forever.*

Mike's wedding vows

Every good and perfect gift comes from the Father. Apart from my salvation, you're the greatest gift that God has ever given me.

You're worth far more than rubies. I have full confidence in you, and I lack nothing of value. You're my best friend. You elevate the meaning of the word friend to such a higher level, that you are my only friend. You are the only person who understands the depth of where I have been, and the magnitude of what God has done for me. I love you.

Ecclesiastes 5:2 (KJV) tells us, "Be not rash with thy mouth, and let not thine heart be hasty to utter anything before God: for God is in Heaven, and thou upon earth: therefore let thy words be few."

Verse 4 and 5 tells us, ⁴"When you make a vow to God, do not delay to pay it, for He has no pleasure in fools. Pay what you have vowed.

⁵Better not to vow, than to vow and not pay."

I'll read my vows often, so that I'm reminded of my promise to you, and my promise to God.

Love and faithfulness never leave me; I bind them around my neck. I write them on the tablet of my heart.

I will give honor to my marriage, and remain faithful to you in marriage.

God gives me grace to love you as Christ loved the church, and also gave Himself for it. I am in agreement with God's will for my life, and the role that He has given me, as your husband.

When I tell you that I love you, I mean that I love you all of the time, without condition, without exception, without expectation, and without reservation.

I will protect you, and I will guard your feelings. I'll lead our family to follow God.

You are my first love, my last love.

Today, on our first day of forever, I promise to you, and I promise to God that I will love you.

We will pray and believe God together.

We will praise and worship God together.

We will honor and glorify His name together.

We will serve God, and promote His kingdom together.

You may be weaker than I am, but you are my equal partner in God's gift of new life.

We will walk together, hand in hand, forever.

It's undeniable that this day is only possible because of God's grace, His mercy, and His unconditional love for us.

We were deaf, blind, bound, broken and buried, but God had a different plan. He's given me life and favor. His visitation has preserved my spirit. His light has pierced the darkness. Our God is faithful and just. He's given us grace to love, and grace for deliverance. He's torn down the walls. He's healed us. He's awakened our souls. He's freed us from bondage. He's given us the truth, and the truth has made us free. He has plans to prosper us, and not to harm us. He's given us hope, and a future. He's restored us. He's redeemed our time. He's taken the impossible, and made it inevitable.

We love God, because He first loved us (First John 4:19 KJV).

To whom much is given, much is required. God's divine order will rule and reign in our lives. His power has come to deliver that which belongs to Him.

We belong to Him. We were bought and paid for with a price. We are the servants of no man.

As for me and my house, we will serve the Lord (Joshua 24:15 KJV).

He does only wondrous things

We had an incredible photographer on site. My best friend was there as my maid of honor, and I was glowing from head to toe. We lit a unity candle, and partook of Holy Communion. The ceremony was filled with God's love and holy inspired prayers. I wore a brand new, long, beautiful wedding gown, gorgeous wedding jewels, including the most brilliant diamond wedding band, and a pair of new shoes with a new purse to match my attire. We had a stunning, tiered wedding cake that was amazingly delicious. Our reception was filled with joy, laughter and celebration. There was an abundance of delicacies and gifts galore. We had a special cutting of our wedding cake, taking our first bites together as we displayed huge nonstop smiles. We had a tremendous amount of help from friends that served us to make everything go so smoothly. We are so blessed to have had such wonderful people there to make that day so special for us. This wedding day, this unimaginable, inconceivable day is well noted as one of the most significant days of my history past.

His banner over me is Love

Looking back at all those hard places that Mike and I had been separated, it's easy now to see how the devil tried to steal from me on every level and at every turn. Thank God, the Lord always prevails over me! His love has never left me. His hand never was completely taken off my life. Sometimes it's extremely difficult to believe that things don't have to be good for God to be glorified, and to work out something good for us. God knew He had a special assignment that He was preparing me for. The devil also knew it. I was the one who knew very little, and had no idea what God was up to. He kept it hidden from me until the appointed time.

He took me through a lifetime of valuable lessons, heartaches and mistakes, and then equipped me to draw from those experiences, so I could handle what the Lord wanted to give back to me. He wanted to bring me back to a place of honor; He wanted to remove the precious from the vile. He wanted to bring me into a place where He knew I would be cherished and loved, but only by His choice of man, not mine. He was making His Word good in my life, and was releasing the *"Restitution"* He promised me back in November of 2013.

Even when Mike and I didn't know we were being set up, God on purpose, aligned all the broken dreams of our shattered lives, and He reunited us. Even in the beginning when we first began communicating, we had absolutely no idea that we would ever be back together, but God had a different plan. Being reunited was the furthest thing from our minds, and it was impossibility on top of impossibility, multiplied to the infinitive degree of the odds of us ever getting back together. The idea of it all would be so impossible, and the very thought of trying to conjure this up goes way beyond my imagination. I couldn't have even dared to dream a dream with those kinds of odds working against me.

There was absolutely no glimmer of hope in my heart *at all* when God began working out His good plan for my life: *Making my life beautiful.* He has graciously rewarded me for obedience to my first love, Jesus Christ, my Lord and Savior.

Who would've known? Who could've seen any of this coming? Neither one of us were in any condition mentally to even entertain a ridiculous thought like we'd ever see each other or be able to trust each other ever again. However; God is God, and His plans and purposes have prevailed. God is a giver. He is good, and He delights to rejoice over His children, and gives them good gifts from above.

Even when it seemed absurd to think that Mike and I could ever be in the same room, and not point fingers and blame toward each other, God saw from Heaven, into the depths of our souls, and helped us see the truth of the matter. He gave us eyes to see purely into each other's heart. It was all according to His time and good pleasure, to bring us back to the happiest place from our youth, and supernaturally made us both better. While neither of us is perfect, the Lord developed and matured us in so many countless ways during the painful process of life's battles.

Another revelation came to me about five months after we had been married. For the first few months of us getting married, I would often cry every time we'd get into a discussion about how thankful we were to be together once again. Since I had recently made the decision to tear up our photos just a few months before we got reconnected, it really bothered me to think that had I not of done that, we'd have those fun photos to look back on today. They ultimately got torn up and thrown away, as I really felt like that's what I was supposed to do at that time. Questions and doubts plagued my mind, tormenting me, wishing I could undo what I did, and somehow get those pictures back. One day it finally made sense to me why those pictures had to be purged. I really believe God led me to destroy those pictures.

With that said, I realize now that if I would have had them, I may have been extremely tempted to get them out, and look at them while we would talk on the phone during the darkest hours of his life. Had that of happened, it's quite possible I would have destroyed the gift he needed most.

What Mike needed most from me initially was not a girlfriend, or even anything that remotely looked, acted or talked like a girlfriend, nor was that my intention. I purposed in my heart daily to be whatever he needed me most to be, and that's the place I ministered to him from. He simply needed someone to point him back to the Cross of Jesus, and convey a message of hope from a God who loved him, and had a good plan and purpose for his life. He needed an uncompromising, spiritually strong and tenacious soldier with a no defeat attitude to pluck him out of the very depths of hell itself.

Greatly humbled, I thank God He used me to help bring Mike deliverance. In doing so, because he chose life, I too, received a brand new, supernatural, bountifully blessed, abundantly-wonderful life. God truly took my mourning, and turned it into joy. He has given me beauty for ashes, and the oil of joy for my gladness. His mercy triumphed over my former shame, despair, despondency and sadness.

And it came to pass

The prophecy I received from the Lord through Pastor Billy Burke on January 9, 2015, did indeed come to pass. I shared this in a previous chapter, but it's worth repeating. In part, the Lord said through him, "He's (God is) about to prosper you beyond your wildest dream," and believe me, He made His word good!

The Lord has raised me up out of the pit of hell. I once lived in gross darkness. Formerly, I was a living soul, but I was a dead woman. He put my feet upon The Rock, Jesus Christ, the One and only true Son of God. He gave me new songs to sing in my heart, songs of deliverance and joy. Jesus Christ took this dead woman's life, and exchanged it for a life of faith, hope and love. He said in His Word, the greatest of these is love. I am a living testament, alive and breathing, that God's love for me is real, and God's love for each one of you is real, too.

His love knows no limits and no boundaries. There's no measurement big enough to measure His unfailing, unconditional, fierce, unstoppable and unquenchable love for each one of us! He delights to do His will in our lives when we seek His face with our whole heart. He delights to do His will for us when we believe in His Son, Jesus Christ. He delights to do His will for us when we are quick to obey His Word, and hearken to His commands. He delights over us with joy, with singing, and with such adoration for His creation and all mankind. He wants you to know that He is actively looking and always pursuing those with hearts of faith, pure in heart, but not necessarily having a perfect performance. He is looking to pour out His Spirit upon each one of you, and as you hear His Word, you shall be healed in the mighty Name of Jesus!

You shall receive an impartation of His great love for you, and see the manifested power of God working all things out together for your good, and to His glory in your lifetime. He desires to mold us into the image of His dear Son. Only believe, dear friend. Only believe! His power is real. His power is hope. His power is healing. His power is restoration and redemption. His blood, the cleansing power of His blood is alive today. His resurrection power is alive, for He is the One and only true living God; He is alive today and forevermore! Hallelujah!

All things, not some, are working together for good

It's quite understandable if my story may be difficult or hard for some to believe, especially the part about the prophetic laugh, or some of the other supernatural events that have shaped my life. I can understand if some are skeptical, I probably would be, too. I recently called my best girlfriend, the one who I was speaking of as the hysterical laugh came upon me, while I was *caught* in the devil's trap. I shared with her that the Lord had finally released revelation to me concerning the interpretation to that prophetic laugh. The meaning is now fully understood, and the enlightenment of my prophetic laugh has been made clear. For decades, the devil *always* had the last laugh on me, causing chaos and havoc in my life, while keeping me emptyhanded and brokenhearted. ***Who do you think God gave the last laugh to?***

Until all these incredibly miraculous things happened to me, I wouldn't have ever thought any of it to be possible. Satan had a plan of entrapment and destruction for my life, but the Holy Spirit led me through a battle marked *"Victory!"* Above all the gifts the Lord gave to me, I am forever grateful that He thought enough of me to give me another chance with my first and only true love. That one man who's void in my heart could be filled by no other. My mind couldn't even conceive such a wonderful gift from Heaven. He gave me an ability to see truth, because His Light pierced my darkness.

In one moment of time, like the snap of a finger, the Lord awakened my soul. God gave me *"Grace to Love"* when I had no ability on my own to do so; *none whatsoever.* He did it on purpose. He did it with a purpose in mind, one much bigger than my imagination, and far beyond my ability to dream. God has proven to me that He wants me to take the limits off. He wants to demonstrate His unfailing love, grace and mercy. He loves to take a life like mine that the devil had stolen, and He absolutely loves to show off the manifestation of His glory and power.

If all these events aren't enough proof that miracles really do happen, there's one more amazing detail of my story that will blow you away, it did me.

Remember I had the mini vision of Mike and me at an alter type setting which came during the triumphant battle for his life? It bothered me a little bit that it seemed backwards, as Mike was on the left, and I was on the right. The Lord revealed to me in His perfect timing, that what I had seen wasn't at all from the audience's perspective. *I was seeing what God saw, since He is the One that really joined us together, not man!*

If all the evidence that God has deliberately given me doesn't prove He loves me, and wants me to be happy, then I don't know what would. The Lord has graciously restored unto me all that the locusts have devoured and destroyed. In due time, He has revealed His glory, and made my life beautiful by giving me beauty for ashes. I am here to testify of His goodness and grace. He safely led me through a lifelong battle, and with love from His heart He said, "My victory is your victory." This is my testimony, and I count it a privilege to share it with you.

May you know there is a God in Heaven who loves and adores you. I pray in the Name of Yeshua HaMashiach that you experience the fullness of His unfailing love, joy, and peace in your life today!

From our first kiss back in 1986, to reuniting at the airport just two days before Valentine's Day of 2015, to Mike's and my fourth engagement, and now... *Finally, Our first day of Forever;* I can't wait to see what's coming next!

...And, concerning the matter of our lives together in marriage, because God did this for us, it's forever. We never had forever, but now we do!

Matthew 19:26 (KJV)

But Jesus beheld [them], and said unto them, "With men this is impossible; but with God all things are possible."

Ecclesiastes 3:14-15 (KJV) says, and we claim His promises today:

[14] *"I know that, whatsoever God doeth, it shall be forever: nothing can be put to it, nor anything taken from it: and God doeth it, that men should fear before Him.*

[15] *That which hath been is now; and that which is to be hath already been; and God requireth that which is past."*

The Light has Pierced the Darkness

Broken dreams; shattered lives. This is what it once was. No hope, failing love.

Destruction and despair all around, surrounding us like a dark cloud.

No sight of Light, no vision to see, but God had a different plan. He had a big dream, bigger than you and me...

He said, "The Light must pierce their darkness. The Light must shine forth.

For without Light they will have no way to see. For their ears must be open to the cry of My heart.

My will shall be performed in Mike and Rhonda's lives. Because I had this dream, I will bring it to pass. It will be glorious. It shall bring Me glory, much glory like no other couple in history past."

"For I shall delight to do My will," saith the Lord of Hosts. "I shall surround them at all times with My presence and power. I shall go before them, and walk in them, and it shall be their pleasure to do My will.

For My plans and My purposes shall be so great that many will shake their heads in dismay and unbelief."

"For My power has come to deliver that which belongs to Me," says the Lord.

"They shall conquer darkness together, equally, jointly together as one in the power of My great love.

For it is My power of love that no man can separate. My eyes shall be open and Mine ears shall be open to the cries of their hearts.

They shall pray and believe Me together. They will know My power, and give Me the glory for all that they accomplish in My Great Name.

My splendor shall be seen in greater measures, because of their obedience to quickly obey with a willing heart.

For I shall make their latter days greater than their former; they shall see the display of My glory and My power manifesting in their daily lives," declares the Lord.

Notes

Chapter Seven: *The Prophetic Voice*

1. *Merriam-Webster's Dictionary, an Encyclopædia Britannica Company,* s.v. *restitution.*

Mike's 18th Birthday!

Rhonda's 16th Birthday!

December 7, 1988
Parris Island S.C.

Who got the last laugh?

Printed in the United States
By Bookmasters